HAPPINESS: FACTS AND MYTHS

HAPPINESS: FACTS AND MYTHS

Michael W. Eysenck
Royal Holloway and Bedford New College
University of London

Lawrence Erlbaum Associates Ltd., Publishers
27 Palmeira Mansions
Church Road
Hove
East Sussex BN3 2FA
U.K.

British Library Cataloguing in Publication Data

Eysenck, Michael W.
   Happiness: facts and myths
   1. Happiness
   I. Title
   152.4

ISBN 0-86377-134-3

Printed and bound by BPCC Wheatons, Exeter

To Christine, Fleur, Willie, Juliet and Maria with love.

Contents

Preface

Numerous popular books on happiness have been published in recent years. The authors of these books make all kinds of weird and wonderful claims about how your life can be transformed as a result of reading their books, since they have discovered the secret (or secrets) of constant happiness. Of course, it would be tremendous if these claims were true, but unfortunately they are not. Simply sitting down and thinking about what is needed for happiness (as most of these authors have done) is most unlikely to produce a book which will be of real use to the unhappy person looking for contentment in his or her life.

This book is quite different from most previous books on happiness in a number of ways. Firstly, it is based fairly and squarely on the scientific evidence about happiness which psychologists have discovered as a result of painstaking research. This means that you are presented with the facts rather than simply speculations. Secondly, I do not make rash claims that there is any simple way of achieving happiness. What I do claim is that a careful reading of this book will provide you with useful insights into the nature and determinants of happiness, and there are also several practical hints which should prove useful in making you happier than you would otherwise have been. Thirdly, I frankly admit that we are far from knowing everything there is to know about happiness. What I have done in this book is to present the current state of knowledge in the hope and belief that you will find it both interesting and helpful.

One of the main messages of the book is that close personal relationships are of especial importance to human happiness. It is thus entirely fitting that this book is dedicated to my family, who have consistently provided me with the love and affection needed to make life a worthwhile and happy experience.

CHAPTER ONE

What is Happiness?

Madame de Gaulle was asked after the death of her husband General de Gaulle what she wanted most during the rest of her life. She was asked the question by an English reporter, and so she gave the answer in English: "Happiness". Unfortunately her English accent was rather fractured, and so the assembled throng gasped at what seemed to be the remarkable Gallic frankness of what she had just said. Since she failed to pronounce the "h" , she appeared to be referring in unambiguous terms to the most distinctive and celebrated part of the male anatomy.

This story illustrates a number of points, apart from the problems of communication that have plagued Anglo-French relations over the centuries. For example, it shows the way in which sex rears its head when the topic of happiness is under discussion. Of greater importance, however, is the fact that most of us would agree with Madame de Gaulle that one of the major goals of life is to be happy. As the great Greek philosopher Aristotle put it: "What is the highest of all goods achievable by action? . . . both the general run of man and people of superior refinement say that it is happiness." The same sentiment finds more contemporary expression in the words of one of the best-selling records of the Liverpool comedian Ken Dodd: "Happiness, happiness, the greatest gift I possess."

Perhaps the greatest testament to the true significance of happiness in the affairs of man is that it was explicitly mentioned as one of man's "unalienable rights" in the second sentence of the American Declaration of Independence: "We hold these truths to be self-evident, that all men are created equal, that they are endowed by their Creator with certain unalienable rights; that among these are, Life, Liberty, and the Pursuit of Happiness."

Nearly everyone is convinced that the pursuit of happiness plays an important part in their lives. However, some philosophers and political thinkers have placed other goals such as personal growth and freedom above it. They have argued that any attempt to creat a Utopian society in which everyone is happy all of the time could succeed

1

only by using techniques of mind control that would be an affront to human dignity. This gloomy view has been endorsed by some novelists, but doesn't make much sense. In fact, people living in free and open societies are on average much happier than those living in oppressive and authoritarian ones.

Happiness is, of course, only one out of a great variety of emotional states, ranging from grief and despair to euphoria and ecstasy. Despite this variety, we can readily describe any given emotional state as good or bad, pleasant or unpleasant. Happiness appears to be the central pleasant emotion. According to one thesaurus, happiness is similar in meaning to a whole string of positive terms, including exhilaration, contentment, bliss, joyfulness, ecstasy, euphoria, pleasure, elation, and optimism.

Anxiety and depression are the major unpleasant or bad emotions. It often seems that contemporary Western society is preoccupied with the unpleasant emotions to the relative exclusion of the more pleasant ones, and that this is the "age of anxiety". This emphasis on anxiety can be seen in the numerous popular books discussing the stresses and strains of everyday life, and attempting to provide a panacea for the anxieties that result. It is true, of course, that the pace of technological change, the threat of nuclear annihilation, the substantial increase in mugging and other types of crime, and numerous other aspects of twentieth century life create genuine stresses, but it may be doubted whether this emphasis on the more negative side of life is really justified. After all, Gallup polls carried out over the years on a nationwide basis in several countries have consistently revealed that at least two-thirds of people are either happy or very happy, and the proportion has not altered much from one decade to the next.

Why, then, does unhappiness in the form of stress and anxiety loom so large in the public consciousness? I hate to admit it (being a psychologist myself), but there are clear indications that psychologists must take some of the responsibility for the prevailing doom and gloom. Psychology textbooks over the past century have devoted approximately twice as much space to the unpleasant emotions as to the pleasant ones, and the imbalance has become much more pronounced in recent years. In terms of books devoted solely to anxiety or to happiness, the discrepancy is truly remarkable. There are literally hundreds of books taking anxiety and stress as their major theme, but a mere handful focussing on happiness. Indeed, it was partly the lack of attention paid to the cheerful and optimistic emotions that prompted the writing of this book.

It is of interest to compare psychologists' treatment of human emotion with that of writers of fiction. In a content analysis of numerous novels, plays, poems, short stories, and quotations, it emerged that virtually three-quarters of the literary references to emotion were pleasant, and the proportion has altered remarkably little over the years. Which specific emotions figure most prominently in fictional works? As you undoubtedly guessed, love heads the list, accounting for one-quarter of all references to emotional experiences. Other positive emotions which have attracted much literary attention are humour (second place overall), happiness (fourth place), and faith (sixth place). The only unpleasant emotions which occupy any of the top six places in the literary content are fear (third place) and horror (fifth place).

If we assume that writers of fiction cater fairly directly to the interests and concerns of their potential audience, then most people are more interested in love and romance than in tragedy and kitchen-sink drama. Why is it that psychologists have been so unresponsive to these preferences? In their defence, psychologists can point to an important but little known characteristic of language: of the thousands of emotion words, almost two-thirds refer to negative or unpleasant emotions. However, it would be quite unwarranted to conclude that people spend most of their time dwelling in misery. Words referring to unpleasant emotions are used less often than those referring to more positive emotions, and this differential usage serves to correct the imbalance. The greater variety of terms to describe negative emotions simply means that more distinctions can be drawn among unpleasant emotions than among pleasant ones.

WHAT IS HAPPINESS?

Our analysis of emotional terms has made it abundantly clear that the pleasant emotions are of crucial significance in human experience, and that psychologists have not devoted sufficient attention to them. In a very modest way, this book attempts to remedy this deficiency, focussing largely on the crucial positive emotion of happiness. We have already discussed briefly what is meant by the term "happiness", but it is now time to explore its meaning more fully. One of the problems is that it is rather vague, and different people use it to mean somewhat different things. According to Aristotle, there are at least three kinds of happiness. At the bottom level, ordinary people have the simple idea that pleasure brings happiness. At a somewhat higher level, those of "superior refinement" equate happiness with doing well. It is interesting to note that Aristotle's observations have a very modern feel about them if we consider popular stereotypes about class differences. Some sociologists argue that working-class or "ordinary" people seek happiness through immediate pleasures such as drinking or watching football, whereas middle-class people (or those of "superior refinement") strive for happiness by attaining long-term goals (e. g., career success).

Aristotle identified a third form of happiness, which he regarded as the highest of them all. This is the happiness which is produced by the contemplative life. Would that we were all lucky enough to be able to escape from the daily pressures of earning a living, bringing up a family, and so on in order to pursue a tranquil life of contemplation! However, it is not at all clear that the contemplative life would suit everyone, particularly those who are naturally dynamic and thrusting.

Views on happiness have changed over the years. Philosophers and other authorities used to claim that durable satisfaction and happiness could be achieved only by pursuing a moral and religious existence. This sort of approach suffers from the grave disadvantage that it tells people what ought to make them happy, rather than paying attention to what does do so. The tide began to turn in the eighteenth century when philosophers such as John Locke and Jeremy Bentham argued that happiness is based on the number of pleasures in one's life. This corresponds more closely to contemporary thinking, and manages to avoid moralistic overtones. In other words, pleasure enhances happiness regardless of whether our pleasure derives from disreputable and reprehensible activities or from noble self-sacrifice. A contemporary view of happiness relates it to pleasures in the form of "satisfied desires". This point of view was expressed by the psychologist Professor McGill: "The root meaning of happiness appears to be something like this: A lasting state of affairs in which the most favourable ratio of satisfied desires to total desires is realized with the proviso that the satisfied desires can include satisfactions that are not preceded by specific desires for them, but come by surprise. Thus we are suddenly delighted by someone's conversation we had not expected to enjoy, yet, if we had not desired the conversation of this kind in the past, we should probably not enjoy it now by surprise." This view of happiness is on the wordy and complicated side. It can be contrasted with the much more succinct definition offered by my daughter Fleur at the age of five. "Happiness", she said, "is love." While many people may feel that my daughter, and countless others who have expressed the same sentiment, have told them all they need to know about happiness, Professor McGill's definition is worth considering in more detail. One of the key issues it raises concerns how to obtain a high ratio of satisfied desires to total desires. There are basically two possible alternatives here: to work hard to make sure that as many as possible of one's desires are actually satisfied, or to reduce the number and complexity of one's desires to a more realistic level.

There is a well-known saying, "The Greeks have a word for it", and so it is no surprise to discover that the ancient Greeks successfully anticipated contemporary thinking, and addressed the very issue posed by Professor McGill's definition. Zeno of Citium founded the Stoic school of philosophy at the end of the fourth century B.C. According to the Stoics, the route to happiness lies in having only a small number of desires, all of which can readily be fulfilled. The opposite position was taken by Aristotle, who among several major achievements was the very first psychologist. He argued that the main way of increasing happiness is to retain all of one's desires, but to put more effort into satisfying them.

Who is right, Zeno or Aristotle? My opinion is that we need to take account of individual differences. Aristotle's preferred strategy may have worked well when he used it himself, and might be appropriate for other clever and competent people. However, many of us may be better advised to take the easy way out and follow Zeno's advice. Personality may also be relevant. Optimists tend to prefer Aristotle's strategy of "going for broke", whereas pessimists are better suited to the more cautious approach advocated by the Stoics.

If you are asked how happy you are, you might answer on the basis of your thoughts about the general trend of your life (e.g., "Everything's going quite smoothly"; "My life is a complete mess"), or you might answer in terms of your current feelings (e.g., "I feel really pleased right now"; "I feel so depressed and low"). If we use "satisfaction" to refer to those thoughts and self-reflections which are related to happiness, and "hedonic level" to refer to the degree to which pleasant emotions outweigh unpleasant ones, then: Happiness = Satisfaction + Hedonic level.

Why should we look at happiness in this way? One major advantage is that it helps us to understand more clearly the deficiencies of some methods of trying to increase happiness. For example, consider drugs such as cocaine, heroin, or "soma" (in Aldous Huxley's Brave New World) which have been used to increase levels of happiness. These drugs may manipulate the user's emotional state so that a heightened hedonic level is achieved, but they generally reduce happiness as reflected in satisfaction with the general course of one's life.

The old saying, "It is better to be an unhappy Socrates than a happy pig," can reasonably be interpreted in the light of the two components of happiness identified above. Pigs (and other animals) may often be happy in the sense of a reasonably high hedonic level, but since they do not assess the success of their previous endeavours in a reflective way they cannot show satisfaction. Thus, one of the disadvantages of being a pig rather than Socrates (there are others which will be obvious to those familiar with the traditional English breakfast) is that a pig can never be happy in the full sense of the term.

If you are asked the question, "Are you happy?", you could answer in terms of your present mood state or of your assessment of your life over the past week, month, or year. In this book, we will deal mainly with happiness over long periods of time, but happiness or euphoria stemming from temporary, very pleasant emotional states will also be considered. After all, how generally happy or unhappy we feel depends importantly on our immediate emotional reactions to the thousands of events which fill our daily lives.

THE TELL-TALE SIGNS

How do we know when someone is happy? It is usually reasonably easy for each of us to decide when we are happy, because we experience the cheerful, joyful, and light-hearted feelings that signal the happy state. Indeed, most people would probably agree that if we do not feel happy, then we are not happy, no matter what those around us may think. In contrast, it can be very difficult to decide whether someone else is happy.

Of course, a happy individual may give voice to his or her state of happiness, talking about feeling "on top of the world", "full of the joys of spring", or "over the moon". Whether or not we should believe someone who tells us they are happy is a moot point. An obvious problem is the so-called "social desirability bias", which simply means that we often distort the truth in order to present a more socially desirable image of ourselves than is actually warranted. For example, most married couples claim that they are very happily married, but the fact that nearly half of them subsequently get divorced suggests that there is some exaggeration in the reported levels of happiness. More powerful evidence for a social desirability bias was obtained in a study in which people completed a questionnaire on happiness either anonymously on their own or in the context of a personal interview. Thirty-six per cent of those interviewed claimed that they were "very happy", against only 23 per cent of those completing the same questionnaire on their own. This difference occurred because the pressures to provide socially desirable answers were greater in the interview situation.

While the existence of the social desirability bias means that we cannot always take someone's claims to be happy at face value, it does not mean that what people tell us about their state of happiness is valueless. When an individual's own rating of his or her level of happiness is compared against an expert rating of that person made by a psychologist, the usual finding is that the two ratings are reasonably close. Thus, listening to what other people tell us about their emotional state usually provides at least partial insight into how they feel, even though there may be an element of distortion involved. More specifically, most people's reports tend to exaggerate somewhat their level of happiness, but they do so to about the same extent. As a consequence, those who report very high levels of happiness are usually genuinely happier than those who report moderately high levels, and so on.

Of course, we do not communicate our feelings only by the words we speak. Non-verbal signals such as facial expression, gesture, posture, eye movements, and tone of voice can all be extremely informative. As far as happiness is concerned, the relevant non-verbal indicators include frequent smiling, an open or non-defensive posture, and a cheerful optimism in the tone of voice. Several popular books such as Manwatching by Desmond Morris have alerted us to the importance of non-verbal signals as a form of communication, but it is still perhaps somewhat puzzling that such signals are needed. After all, there are approximately half a million words in the English language, so presumably almost any subtle feeling can be expressed verbally. Why then has the "silent language" of non-verbal signals developed? According to Michael Argyle of Oxford University, language and non-verbal signals are designed to fulfil different functions. Since we often do not want to express our feelings too directly and publicly, we resort to non-verbal signals, which have the advantage of being more ambiguous than spoken language. In contrast, language communicates information about people and events external to the speaker.

So far, so good. There appear to be several aspects of behaviour which reflect internal happy states, and non-verbal signals are more likely than verbal ones to be used to convey emotion. It looks as if it should be quite easy to decide whether or not someone else is happy. A complicating factor is that most societies lay great emphasis on behaving in a pleasant and agreeable way. There are usually strong pressures on people to put a good face on things, and to avoid moaning and grumbling about their misfortunes. As the old saying goes, "Laugh, and the world laughs with you; weep, and you weep alone."

Given the cultural expectation that unhappiness should be hidden from public gaze, it follows that unhappy people will often attempt to mimic the behaviour patterns of those who are genuinely happy. How can we detect such deception? Conventional wisdom as expressed by Desmond "The Naked Ape" Morris and others tells us that people can control the verbal but not the non-verbal components of their behaviour. This point of view dates back at least to the originator of psycho-analysis, Sigmund Freud, who described the deceiver in the following graphic way: "If his lips are silent, he chatters with his fingertips; betrayal oozes out of him at every pore."

Of course, anyone can say "I feel really happy" whether they actually mean it or not, whereas it may seem that it would be harder to manipulate non-verbal behaviour to convey the desired effect. This is more true of some forms of non-verbal behaviour than others. For example, we tend to be more aware of our facial expressions than of our body movements, and we also find it relatively easy to control our facial muscles. Thus, in spite of the great importance we assign to facial expression when interpreting someone else's emotional state, the face actually can provide very misleading information. Despite this, the face of someone who is feigning happiness does actually give tell-tale clues to that person's true emotional state, and experienced facial analysts are able to make accurate use of these clues. The clues take the form of micro-expressions. They are extremely brief muscular movements which are the remnants of the true emotional state. These micro-expressions are so brief, indeed, that their existence was confirmed only when films of face were shown in slow motion.

Hamlet observed that "One may smile, and smile, and be a villain." What Hamlet did not go on to say, however, was that smiling is more likely to mask true feelings in women than in men. Traditionally, women's social role has tended to involve submissiveness and warmth to a greater extent than that of men, and smiling has therefore been very much part and parcel of the way women have been expected to behave. Before I get shot, I should point out that the advent of feminism has had marked effects both here and elsewhere. Nevertheless, it was found in a recent study that the father's smile is more informative than that of the mother. When fathers smile at their children, they are usually saying something friendlier or more approving than when they are not smiling. Rather surprisingly, mothers smiling at their children are just as likely to be saying something unfriendly as mothers who are not smiling. It also turns out that the presence of psychologists with their film cameras dramatically increases the amount of smiling of mothers interacting with their children. This shows how social pressures can affect non-verbal behaviour, with mothers being more likely to adopt the stereotyped role of the warm, smiling mother figure when other people are watching. We have seen that the face is not a very reliable indicator of someone's true emotional state, and also that the same is true of the words that are spoken. This brings us back to the question of how we know whether someone is happy or not. Matters are complicated by the fact that there are cultural rules dictating the appropriate mode of expression for happiness in any particular situation. Punching the air, jumping up and down, shouting, and singing are acceptable ways of indicating happiness at a football match when the side you support is winning, but might not go down as well when you have just beaten someone at tennis.

The various cultural rules apply mainly to body language, which leaves tone of voice as the final measure of happiness that we need to consider. We can hear ourselves speak, but as anyone who has heard their own voice on tape will probably agree, we actually hear a very distorted version of it. What is perhaps less well-known is that most people have rather poor control over their tone of voice, unless they have followed the practice of a number of actors and leading politicians and had special voice training. Thus, the best indicator of a person's emotional state is tone of voice: decide whether the person sounds happy rather than focussing too much on whether he or she looks happy.

One useful strategy when trying to decide what another person is really feeling is to decide whether all of the available evidence is conveying the same message. So far as happiness is concerned, the message should indicate zest and enthusiasm, since the great philosopher Bertrand Russell was probably right when he claimed that zest is "the most universal and distinctive mark of the happy man." Therefore, we must ask whether the other person is really behaving with zest and gusto. If the signals are inconsistent, then in all probability the other person is not truly happy. Thus, for example, if someone has a happy face but says something that is not very friendly, this probably indicates submissiveness or insincerity, whereas pleasant things said by someone whose facial expression does not reveal happiness indicate sarcasm.

A final rule of thumb that may prove helpful in assessing someone's true feelings is that people who are feigning happiness are more likely to change their behaviour too much rather than too little. As a result, we have the paradoxical state of affairs that the deceiver's attempts to control his or her behaviour often provides the best cues to deception. "Happy" external behaviour that appears planned, rehearsed, and lacking in spontaneity usually masks an unhappy individual within.

PEAK EXPERIENCES

A useful way of clarifying our ideas on happiness is to consider relatively pure or extreme examples of the happy state. We all know which of life's experiences have produced the greatest joy and ecstasy for us, but we probably have only a hazy idea of what most other people regard as their personal moments of greatest happiness. Before the so-called "sexual revolution", it was often argued that maximal happiness could be attained through certain religious experiences. One or two writers of the past even went so far as to put forward the astonishing claim that all happiness has a religious basis, as in this quotation from William James, the psychologist brother of the writer Henry James: "In all countries and in all ages, some form of physical enlargement—singing, dancing, drinking, sexual excitement—has been intimately associated with worship. Even the momentary expression of the soul in laughter is, to however slight an extent, a religious exercise."

While it is easy to scoff at these bizarre and out-dated views, there is no doubt that religion used to be of great importance in determining people's attitudes and feelings. Several examples of the powerful emotions triggered off by religious conversion experiences were recorded at the turn of the century by William James. The flavour of such experiences is captured in one man's description of what happened to him when he was on top of a hill late one night: "I stood alone with Him who had made me, and all the beauty of the world, and love, and sorrow, and even temptation. I did not seek Him, but felt that perfect unison of my spirit with His. The ordinary sense of things around me faded. For the moment nothing but an ineffable joy and exaltation remained ... It was like the effect of some great orchestra when all the separate notes have melted into one swelling harmony that leaves the listener conscious of nothing save that his soul is being wafted upwards, and almost bursting with its own emotion . . . I could not any more have doubted that He was there than that I was."

Over 50 years later, the psychologist Abraham Maslow carried out a more systematic investigation of the experiences which people have that stand out in the memory because of the tremendous happiness and joy associated with them. Maslow and others have described these all-too-rare moments as "peak experiences". These experiences have been defined by Marganita Laski as being "joyful, transitory, unexpected, rare, valued, and extraordinary to the point of often seeming as if derived from a preternatural source."

Abraham Maslow embarked on his study of peak experiences with the advantage that he had first-hand acquaintance with them. In his own words, "I had lots of them, I remember. I think I used to call it 'exultation' to myself, with lump in throat, tears in eyes, chills, prickles, slight feeling of (pleasant) nausea, and sorts of other autonomic reactions plus impulse to shout and yell." He confessed that he found it rather embarrassing to reveal his peak experiences to the public, but he did admit that he was profoundly affected by classical music. Of all composers, Bach produced more peak experiences for him than any other, with Brahms and Beethoven also being high on the list.

When Maslow asked 190 people to describe their peak experiences, he found that many peak experiences had a somewhat mystical feel to them. However, there were relatively few specifically religious experiences. The two most frequent ways of having peak experiences were through sex and music. Other factors that were often mentioned were the achievement of real excellence or perfection, and women reported peak experiences from the birth of their children. What is particularly striking is that peak experiences occur under a great variety of different circumstances.

In spite of this diversity, there are certain general trends running through the descriptions of peak experiences. There is typically a disorientation in time and space, almost as if the person having a peak experience is outside of space and time. There is also a fusion of the experiencer with the situation, producing a loss of self. Often there is passive acceptance of what is happening, rather along the lines of the Taoistic philosophers of the East with their notion of "let be". Peak experiences tend to have a mystical quality that is described as "cosmic" or "ecstasy". Finally, in peak experiences the nature of reality is seen much more clearly than usual, and its essence is penetrated more profoundly.

Many philosophers and theologians have used these characteristics of peak experiences to argue that the world is good, and that pain, evil, and misery result from the fact that we normally see the world in a very limited and partial way. Indeed, Abraham Maslow himself firmly believed that peak experiences should be regarded as genuine revelations of reality. If we could accept this viewpoint, then this would obviously endow peak experiences with huge significance. It is certainly true that people having a peak experience often feel that they have been granted a glimpse of the essential nature of the universe, but it is entirely possible that they are deluded. A proper scepticism in such matters was expressed by William James: "What immediately feels most 'good' is not always most 'true' when measured by the verdict of the rest of experience . . . The difference between Philip drunk and Philip sober is the classic instance in corroboration. If merely 'feeling good' could decide, drunkenness would be the supremely valid human experience. But its revelations, however acutely satisfying at the moment, are inserted into an environment which refuses to bear them out for any length of time."

AGE AND SEX

Our focus so far has been on the kinds of events and experiences that make adults especially happy. We all know, however, that people vary in the things which give them pleasure and enjoyment. A very important factor here is age, since clearly the pleasures of childhood are by no means the same as those of adolescence or middle age. Another factor worth considering is sex or gender, because there is much evidence that men and women enjoy different activities (although the continuation of the species suggests that there is at least one major joint activity they both enjoy!).

Edward Scott addressed these issues in a major study a few years ago. He started out by asking 70 eleven-year-old boys and an equal number of girls in Portland, Oregon, in North America to describe in some detail the happiest event that had happened to them. Approximately one-third described a special family outing, and lots of children mentioned a specific Christmas or birthday present. One girl described her happiest event in the following way: "When I lived in Albany I had my very, very, very best friends I've ever had, cause we stayed all night at their house. I had them over. We played and at night we had Kool Aide. You name it, we had it."

The unfortunately-named Mrs. Looney was a teacher of eleven-year-old children, and she asked them to define happiness. The answers she received reveal quite well the preoccupations of children of that age. One boy suggested "When somebody turns the clock ahead when you are at school," and a girl said "Going to bed after your brother."

The most interesting aspect of happiness among eleven-year-olds is the fact that sex differences are already apparent. None of the girls studied by Scott referred to personal achievement when describing their happiest event, whereas 20 per cent of the boys did. On the other hand, 10 per cent of the girls had experienced their happiest event through the friendship of others, but this was not true for any of the boys.

The same general picture emerged when the children were asked which problems presented the greatest obstacle to their happiness. Four times as many of the boys as of the girls mentioned poor marks or grades at school, whereas twice as many girls as boys referred to interpersonal problems with other children of the same age. Thus, even at the tender age of eleven, many of the traditional sex differences in cultural expectations have already been assimilated. These findings are pretty much in line with what feminists would have predicted, and there does seem to be some merit in their argument that little girls are "brainwashed" into preferring the role of home-maker to that of bread-winner.

The turbulent years of adolescence are usually regarded as a period of rapid change and development in which attitudes, feelings, and behaviour are all transformed. Edward Scott endeavoured to see whether adolescence had as great an impact on people's happiest events. The answers he received from 140 unmarried university students fitted in well with the stereotypes that men should be strong and stand on their own two feet, whereas women should attach particular importance to successful interpersonal relationships. Forty per cent of the men described some great personal achievement as their happiest event, and a further 17 per cent referred to an event that made them feel self-confident or independent. Among the female students, only a modest 13 per cent regarded a personal achievement as their happiest event, with another four per cent describing an event that produced self-confidence.

As might be expected on the basis of the responses of the eleven-year-olds, the female students were much more likely than the male students to think of some social or interpersonal event when asked to consider their happiest event. Twenty-seven per cent of the women cited a romantic encounter as their happiest event (versus 11 per cent of the men), and 16 per cent of them described a family event such as a marriage or the birth of a sibling (against only 9 per cent of the men). Thus, the tendencies towards differences between male and female happiest events in line with cultural stereotypes which are discernible at the age of 11 become clearer and more marked at the age of 20.

We have spent some time considering the rather dry figures of percentages of male and female students reporting different categories of happiest events. Let us now bring these bald statistics to life by reporting two descriptions of their happiest event, the first being given by a female student and the second by a male student. The descriptions illustrate vividly the different ways in which young men and women find happiness: "When my boyfriend and I were in the park on see-saws I had so much fun. That was a happy time. A very happy time. Not because I received a gift or got a four point on my report card, but happy because I was with someone I love, and it was such a simple spontaneous time. We laughed and laughed."

In contrast, here is a male perspective on happiness that is strongly reminiscent of *Easy Rider*: "The day I left for Colorado in my red and white Rambler station wagon. I think the happy thing was that I was entirely on my own and was free in a sense from all events around me. This allowed me to go and do as I pleased."

Finally, Edward Scott explored happiness among 140 married people. Not surprisingly, marriage or the birth of a child formed the happiest event for well over half of the sample. Typical of the descriptions given by married women of their happiest event is the following: "The minute when my baby was put in my arms. The thought that a new life was partly my doing was breath-taking. The warmth and smell of that body gave me an indescribable feeling of joy—here was living proof of love."

The married man's perspective can be illustrated by this account of one man's happiest event: "Not on the first day of marriage but later, during a sort of honeymoon following a period of absence due to being in the service. My wife and I focussed our attention upon one another almost to the point of excluding everything else, gave no thought to our responsibilities to the past, or to the future, intensely appreciating the present which was in our immediate grasp—an existential experience. It lasted about ten days and nights."

One of the most fascinating aspects of the findings of Edward Scott and of other investigators is the immense variety and range of events that can produce the peaks of happiness and euphoria. Supreme happiness can be associated with listening to music or making love, and can range from driving a station wagon to religious conversion, and from having a baby to riding a see-saw. Is it possible to discern any pattern running through all of these diverse events? What they seem to have in common is that they represent the satisfaction of some powerful desire. Most of us want to be loved, to have a blissful marriage, and so on, and the successful accomplishment of any powerful desire usually produces great happiness and contentment. Thus, our detailed consideration of the happiest events or peak experiences in people's lives has provided a measure of support for Immanuel's Kant's view that happiness consists of "the satisfaction of all our desires."

Peak experiences can help to make life worthwhile, but they suffer from the rather sad and unfortunate characteristic that they tend to be short-lived. A crumb of comfort was provided by the American poet Robert Frost in the title of one of his best-known poems: "Happiness makes up in height for what it lacks in length." It is also worth remembering that happiness depends not only upon a high level of positive affect or emotion, but also upon a more reflective assessment of overall satisfaction with one's life. Very positive emotional states may tend to be of short duration, but satisfaction can be long-lasting, and thus may be a more realistic goal of human existence.

CHAPTER TWO

Who is Happy?

Why are some people happier than others? The most popular answer to that question is that people who have lots of money, a good family life, good health, and are successful in their careers are most likely to be happy. In contrast, those who are poor, have no family, poor health, and no job or an unskilled job are least likely to be happy. There is an element of truth in the popular view. However, in this chapter I will be adopting a different, and somewhat controversial, viewpoint, according to which happiness depends in large measure on the personality that an individual happens to be born with. Thus, there are some lucky people who naturally have a "sunny" disposition, whereas others are destined to spend most of the time grumbling and complaining about their lot.

In essence, the world can be divided into two large categories: the optimists and the pessimists. For the optimists, the glass is half full; for the pessimists, the glass is half empty. But, you may protest, the level of happiness is determined by an individual's experiences rather than by his or her personality. You may be happy at home because you have a loving family, but unhappy at work because you have an uninteresting and poorly paid job. Happiness in some aspects of life combined with unhappiness in others can hardly be accounted for by assuming that every person is naturally happy or unhappy.

It is true, of course, that individual differences in happiness depend importantly on the experiences we have, and there is no doubt that our lives can be enhanced by good luck or ruined by bad luck. However, it is also true that, to a greater or lesser extent, we make our own luck in this life. Thus, a person may have a happy family life because he is a friendly and caring person who inspires love in his wife and children, rather than because he has been lucky. There is fairly general agreement to the proposition that an individual's personality and his or her experiences through life both have key roles to play in determining that individual's overall level of happiness. However, I want to argue that happiness stems mainly from personality.

EMOTIONAL STATES

If we are to understand how personality relates to happiness, it is useful to consider the range of human emotions to see where happiness fits in. A problem is that at first glance (and probably at second glance, too) the whole field of emotion looks like a psychologist's nightmare. There is a vast number of different emotional states, ranging from euphoria to disgust, and from terror to boredom. When a group of researchers worked their way laboriously through thousands of English words describing emotion, they finished up with the staggering total of 558 different concepts referring to temporary emotional states. How on earth can the poor psychologist, whose job it is to impose order on apparent chaos, succeed in reducing the subtleties and richness of emotional experience to manageable proportions?

It is often said that there are more questions than answers. Here we have a counter-example, because literally dozens of answers have been proposed to the above question. A particularly influential answer was provided by the father of experimental psychology, Wilhelm Wundt. He claimed that all feelings or emotions can be assigned a location somewhere within a three-dimensional framework incorporating the dimensions of pleasantness-unpleasantness, excitation-inhibition, and strain-relaxation.

John B. Watson, the founder of a school of psychology known as Behaviourism, agreed with Wundt that a crucial aspect of emotional experiences is whether they are pleasant or unpleasant. Perhaps influenced by his pioneering attempts to investigate sexuality scientifically under laboratory conditions, he proposed that the tumescence occurring during sexual activity is the prototype for all pleasant feelings, whereas the subsequent detumescence is the model for unpleasant feelings. It is not altogether clear from this account where children's emotional states are supposed to come from.

A modern view of how different emotions relate to each other was offered recently by James Russell of the University of British Columbia in Vancouver. He proposed the straightforward view that all emotions can be defined in terms of their locations on the two dimensions of pleasure-displeasure and arousal. This view may sound like a gross over-simplification, but inspection of Fig. 1 reveals that a great variety of emotional terms can be defined fairly precisely as some combination of arousal level (which is a measure of intensity) and also of pleasure-displeasure (which is a measure of emotional quality). As you look round the circle, you will probably agree that words which are adjacent to each other do, in fact, refer to very similar emotional states. Thus, "tired" and "sleepy" closely resemble each other, but it is marginally more pleasurable to be "sleepy" than to be "tired". Similarly, "content" and "glad" describe similar states, but being "glad" is slightly more arousing and pleasurable than being "content".

We now come to a feature of this model of emotion which apparently deviates from common sense. It is natural to assume that positive emotional states (or positive affect in psychologists' jargon) are simply the opposite of negative emotional states (or negative affect). However, a closer examination of the evidence points to a rather different conclusion. In terms of Russell's model, intense positive emotional states or positive affect are characterized by pleasure, but they derive their intensity from high

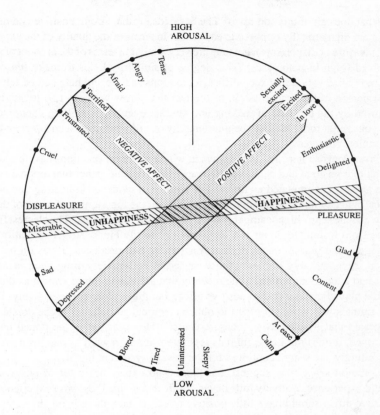

FIG.1 Two-dimensional structure of mood states

arousal. As is shown in Fig. 1, the strongest positive affect thus falls in the quadrant containing pleasurable, high arousal emotional states; these include being in love, excited, delighted, enthusiastic, and sexually excited. The other end of the positive affect dimension naturally consists of terms that describe a relative absence of any positive affect. These terms include tired, bored, uninterested, and depressed, all of which lie in the quadrant consisting of displeasurable, low arousal emotions. Thus, the opposite of strong positive affect is weak positive affect rather than strong negative affect.

A very similar picture presents itself when we turn to the various negative emotional states that comprise negative affect. The most intense negative affect stems from the unfortunate combination of displeasure and high arousal, and encompasses various emotional terms such as terrified, hostile, angry, frustrated, fearful, and cruel. The opposite end of the negative affect dimension lies in the quadrant of pleasurable, low arousal emotional states such as content, calm, and at ease.

What does all of this add up to? The basic idea is that strong positive and negative affect are diametrically opposed to each other in terms of the quality of the experience (i.e., pleasure or displeasure), but they are very similar in terms of the amount of arousal involved (high in both cases). This degree of similarity helps to make sense of the common observation that such different emotions as love and hate can be felt for the same person in rapid succession, or the fact that a row between two lovers is often followed by the pleasure of making up. Another even more striking phenomenon is that you are far more likely to be murdered by one of your nearest and dearest than by a complete stranger.

Physiologists interested in the ways in which the brain functions have pursued the notion that positive and negative affect are quite separate rather than opposites. They have already accumulated an impressive amount of evidence indicating that negative affect (or at any rate anxiety) depends crucially on the functioning of a part of the brain known as the septo-hippocampal system. How do they know this? The clearest findings come from lesions to either the septal area or to the hippocampal formation. Such damage to the brain reduces normal functioning and produces effects on behaviour which are remarkably similar to those caused by anti-anxiety drugs such as alcohol.

It had been thought until quite recently that a brain structure known as the dorsal bundle played a major role in positive affect, but this no longer seems likely. The fact that animals will work very hard to obtain electrical stimulation of the dorsal bundle suggested that it acted as a "pleasure centre". However, when the dorsal bundle is destroyed, it does not make animals less interested in reward as had been predicted. Accordingly, the search continues for the reward system in the brain.

Common sense may suggest that those who experience a lot of positive affect should experience relatively little negative affect, and that those who experience much negative affect should have little positive affect. In fact, there is much evidence that positive and negative affect are quite unrelated to each other, rather than being opposite sides of the same coin. How can we explain this puzzling state of affairs? Peter Warr and his colleagues at the University of Sheffield in England have provided part of the answer. They argued with impeccable logic that positive affect is produced by pleasant events or experiences, whereas negative affect is generated by unpleasant events or experiences. They found that there was practically no relationship between the numbers of nice and nasty things that happened to people, and this is what produces the lack of a relationship between positive and negative affect. We may sometimes feel that people are either generally lucky (i.e., many pleasant experiences and very few unpleasant ones) or generally unlucky (i.e., few pleasant experiences and many unpleasant ones), but the reality is otherwise.

We have now constructed a kind of sketch-map of human emotional experiences. Where does happiness fit into it? It is blindingly obvious that happiness depends in large measure on positive affect, but it also involves a relative absence of negative affect. In other words, in order to be happy what you must do is to "accentuate the positive, eliminate the negative." The location of the happiness dimension within James Russell's model is shown in Fig. 1.

The American psychologist Norman Bradburn confirmed this point of view. He discovered that he could predict someone's reported happiness or subjective well-being by calculating the discrepancy between their levels of positive and negative affect. In other words, happiness is the sum of pleasures minus pains. This measure was more closely related to happiness than the level of positive affect or negative affect considered on its own.

If happiness consists of a blend of high positive affect and low negative affect, then unhappiness is a mixture of high negative affect and low positive affect. This way of looking at unhappiness may help to shed light on a controversy that has dogged clinical psychology. It has generally been assumed that there are two major neurotic mood disorders, anxiety and depression. However, since many anxious patients are depressed, and depressed patients are often anxious, some authorities have concluded that anxiety and depression are almost identical. It is undeniable that groups of depressed and anxious patients are both very unhappy, but the contributions of negative and positive affect to unhappiness may well differ. Depression is an unhappy state involving very low positive affect, with the future looking bleak and unrewarding. In contrast, anxiety is an unhappy state in which there is extremely high negative affect. The anxious person is worried, but can nevertheless perceive the possibility of future happiness, and so experiences a reasonable amount of positive affect.

DIMENSIONS OF PERSONALITY

It is time to consider further how individual differences in personality influence our level of happiness. Personality theorists over the ages have put forward a very large number of different personality dimensions covering virtually all possible motivational and emotional states. Despite this diversity, the task of deciding which personality dimensions are primarily involved in condemning us to unhappiness or alternatively offering us prolonged happiness is simplified by the reasonably good agreement among experts that two personality dimensions are of particular importance. My father, Hans Eysenck, labelled these two dimensions extraversion-introversion and neuroticism-stability many years ago; they are shown in Fig. 2.

Of course, most people tend to have personalities which are not extreme, and so in a sense the "normal" individual would be someone who was neither introverted nor extraverted, and neither neurotic nor completely stable. Nevertheless, many people's personalities are relatively extreme in one way or another, and you probably know some people who are the "life and soul of the party" and others who are rather quiet.

The typical extravert is someone who is sociable, impulsive, lively, and excitable. He or she enjoys company, and likes to go to a lot of parties. In terms of well-known real and fictional figures, David Frost, Mel Brooks, Peter Ustinov, and Falstaff are all rather extraverted. On the other hand, the typical introvert is reserved, thoughtful, controlled, and serious. Ex-President Richard Nixon, Sir Geoffrey Howe, and Sherlock Holmes all appear to qualify as introverts.

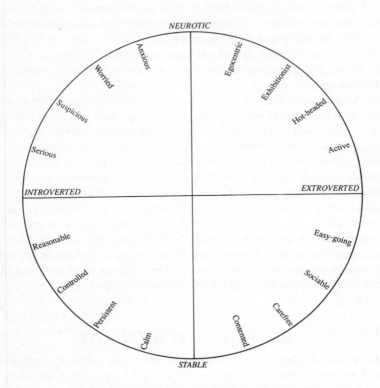

FIG.2 Two-dimensional structure of personality

If we turn to the other personality dimension, then neurotic people tend to be anxious, worried, and very changeable emotionally, whereas stable people are relatively calm, contented, and unemotional. We can perhaps identify examples of these two extremes in the world of professional tennis. John McEnroe has certainly had one or two neurotic moments, whereas Chris Evert seems to be calm and very stable.

This two-dimensional model manifestly fails to capture all of the richness of human personality. However, it has proved remarkably successful in accounting for individual differences in self-reported happiness. What the model basically provides us with are four main personality types formed by the combination of extraverted or introverted, and neurotic or stable. It is rather surprising and intriguing to discover that almost precisely this way of looking at personality was first put forward almost 2000 years ago by the Greek physician Galen. He identified four temperaments which he called the choleric, sanguine, phlegmatic, and melancholic. Each of these temperaments was thought to depend on a different humour or body fluid. This notion of humours has died the death, but it still seems reasonable to distinguish four basic temperaments.

Nowadays those whom Galen described as choleric would be called neurotic extraverts, with sanguine people being stable extraverts, melancholics being neurotic introverts, and phlegmatics being stable introverts.

There has been a certain amount of dispute as to whether people really possess a particular personality or temperament. After all, you may be extraverted when you go to parties but relatively introverted at work. In the same way, you may well feel stable and unemotional some of the time, but neurotic and anxious when confronting a major problem. It is beyond dispute that how we act and feel does depend on the particular situation, and few people are either always extraverted or introverted. However, despite a certain amount of variation from situation to situation, there is still overwhelming evidence for a reasonable amount of consistency in the behaviour and feelings of most people. For example, some people remain calm and collected even under severe pressure, whereas others are inclined to panic and become anxious and agitated at the smallest problem. Thus, the only fair conclusion seems to be that people generally behave in consistent and predictable ways in line with their personalities, but certain situations or events may cause them to "act out of character".

Particularly striking evidence that personality is genuinely consistent and enduring comes from assessing personality at different points in someone's life. From knowing what a person's personality was like at the age of 20, does this allow us to predict what their personality will be like 10, 20, 30, or even 40 years later? The answer is a resounding "yes". Most people's personalities remain rather constant throughout adult life, but some people show more constancy than others. Attitudes and opinions frequently alter dramatically over the years, and the activities that an individual is involved in also tend to change. Nevertheless, he or she tends to remain introverted or extraverted, stable or neurotic. The major exceptions to this generalization occur when an individual is exposed to extreme circumstances, such as during a period of war or following bereavement. Even the most stable person would have been hard pressed to remain calm and unanxious if he had spent four years in the trenches during the First World War.

Nature and Nurture

How is it that the majority of people exhibit the consistency of behaviour over the years that we perceive as their personality? Broadly speaking, there are two main possibilities. According to the environmental theory, each one of us is brought up in a somewhat different environment, and it is the impact of that environment which makes us what we are. Thus, for example, an only child who has relatively little contact with other children while he or she is growing up may develop into an introvert, whereas a child from a large and gregarious family will be more likely to become an extravert. According to the alternative theory, introverts and extraverts, neurotics and stables, are born rather than made.

There is some truth in both theoretical positions. The seeds of personality are laid down in the genes, but adult personality is often affected greatly by the experiences that an individual has had during childhood and afterwards. Heredity and environment are of roughly comparable importance in influencing personality, but with heredity making a somewhat greater contribution. The most crucial part of the evidence comes from studying identical twins brought up in different families. As you might imagine, identical twins brought up apart are rather thin on the ground, but appeals through radio and television have helped psychologists to uncover a reasonable number of them.

Identical twins brought up apart are of great importance because those who believe in nature and those who favour nurture have entirely different predictions to make about how similar their personalities should be. Those who favour nurture would assume that the fact that the twins have grown up in quite different environments means that their personalities will be no more similar than pairs of children selected at random. In contrast, those who believe in nature point to the fact that both twins have essentially identical heredity, and conclude that the twins should be very similar in personality despite the differences in family and social environment.

The evidence strongly supports those who emphasize the role of nature in personality, because identical twins are generally rather similar in personality. There are some reported cases of identical twins brought up apart where the similarities are quite spooky. James Springer, a record clerk in Dayton, Ohio, did not see his identical twin James Lewis, a security guard in Lima, Ohio, for 39 long years. Despite this, they had (unknown to each other) both spent holidays at the same small beach in Florida, and they had both driven there and back in the same make of car (Chevrolet). James Lewis and James Springer had both married a girl Linda as their first wife, and then married someone called Betty. Finally, they both suffered from headaches that started shortly after lunch and developed into migraine, they both suffered from haemorrhoids, and they had both had two heart attacks.

THE "HAPPINESS GENE"

Having established that genetic factors are of major significance in determining personality, we are now in a position to embark on a quest for the "happiness gene". The possessor of this hypothetical gene would need to have great potential for experiencing positive affect combined with relative immunity to negative affect. In contrast, an individual saddled with the "unhappiness gene" would be very receptive to negative affect but almost unaffected by positive affect. The two intrepid explorers who recently made the big breakthrough are Paul Costa and Robert McCrae of Baltimore, Maryland in the United States of America. They managed to track down the personality dimensions primarily associated with positive and negative affect.

Costa and McCrae discovered that it is extraverts who experience the most positive affect, and introverts who least often experience positive affect. Since extraversion consists of different aspects such as sociability and impulsiveness, they went on to identify that aspect most closely related to positive affect. It turned out that it is sociability or the enjoyment derived from the company of other people that is largely responsible for extraverts' high level of positive affect. This makes a lot of sense, since it is obvious that much of the pleasure in life comes from the love, friendship, sympathy, and understanding which other people can share with us. Not surprisingly, there is plentiful evidence that positive affect is strongly related to the frequency of contact with friends and relations, making new friends, and involvement in social organizations. The disinclination of introverts to have numerous social contacts seems to prevent them from experiencing much of the excitement and delight associated with high positive affect.

The notion that extraverts experience more positive affect than introverts mainly because of their greater involvement in social situations has been convincingly shown by Ed Diener in the United States. He asked introverted and extraverted students to wear a special wristwatch with an alarm mechanism which emitted a sound at irregular intervals. Whenever they heard the sound, they were to note down the situation they were in and indicate how much positive affect they were experiencing at that moment. When they were in social situations, the extraverted students reported much more positive affect than the introverted students. However, when they were working or just on their own, there was much less difference in the level of positive affect between the extraverts and the introverts.

The picture with respect to negative affect is even clearer. Those unfortunate individuals who are high in neuroticism or anxiety are plagued by negative affect to a much greater extent than stable individuals. Indeed, so strong is the impact of neuroticism on mood that even when sitting quietly in unstressed conditions neurotic or anxious people are still more discontented than their stable counterparts! This indicates that negative affect does not occur simply as a reaction to unpleasant events such as failing to obtain a desired job, or the ending of a relationship.

Neurotic people often delude themselves by thinking, "I would be so happy if only I weren't worried about X." However, what typically happens is that as soon as X (e.g., an important examination; an interview for a job) is out of the way, a whole lot of worries which had been pushed aside by worry about X suddenly start rearing their ugly heads and looming larger. In other words, some people are naturally worriers and are thus susceptible to negative affect almost regardless of what happens in their lives, whereas others somehow manage to cope with most of the vicissitudes of life with calmness and a lack of fear.

Andrew Mathews, Colin MacLeod, and I have recently had a closer look at people high and low in anxiety. It turns out that they differ dramatically in the ways in which they handle threat. Those who are highly anxious typically select out and process mildly threatening stimuli even when they are not consciously aware that a stimulus has been presented at all. In contrast, those low in anxiety react to threatening stimuli in a much more defensive fashion, selectively avoiding them whenever possible. The tendency of the anxious to seize on mildly threatening stimuli obviously makes the environment seem rather threatening to them, whereas those low in anxiety are protected from some of the minor threats of life, and are more relaxed and unstressed as a result.

In everyday life we frequently encounter ambiguous situations which may or may not pose a genuine threat. For example, if you hear a strange noise in your house at the dead of night, it may be caused by a burglar or there may be a perfectly innocuous explanation. Those who are highly anxious tend to interpret such ambiguous events in a threatening way. In other words, they tend to fear the worst. On the other hand, those who are low in anxiety usually assume that all is well, and need much persuasion that something threatening is happening. These differences in the interpretation of ambiguity also help to explain why people who are high in anxiety experience so much negative affect.

We have seen that extraversion makes a major contribution to one's positive enjoyment of life, whereas neuroticism or anxiety predisposes one to suffer more deeply from life's misfortunes. In addition, extraversion does not afford protection against the negative affect caused by adverse and stressful circumstances. On a more cheerful note, neuroticism or anxiety does not prevent one from enjoying life's pleasures.

Since happiness consists of a combination of high positive affect and low negative affect, we are now in a position to identify with some confidence the possessors of the "happiness gene". These lucky individuals are the stable extraverts with their sanguine temperament. Their extraversion generates much positive affect and their stability or low neuroticism stops them from suffering overly from negative affect and the slings and arrows of outrageous fortune. The unfortunate and wretched possessors of the "unhappiness gene" are the neurotic introverts or melancholics. They really seem to have been singled out by an unkind fate, because their introversion curbs their enjoyment of life, and their neuroticism makes them especially prone to anxiety and negative affect.

This leaves us with two personality types that have not been discussed in relation to happiness. What about stable introverts and neurotic extraverts? Both kinds of personality have similar, intermediate levels of happiness, but what is intriguing is that they achieve this end result in very different ways. Stable introverts or phlegmatics experience little negative affect because they are stable or non-neurotic, and they also rarely feel much positive affect because of their introversion. Thus, stable introverts are seldom either "down in the dumps" or "on top of the world". In vivid contrast, neurotic extraverts or cholerics live life on an emotional roller-coaster. They experience both the highs and the lows emotionally, but their moods average out at a moderate level of happiness. What is of further interest about phlegmatics and cholerics is that both illustrate clearly that high positive affect does not necessarily imply low negative affect, nor does low positive affect invariably go with high negative affect.

INTELLIGENCE

Of course, individuals differ from each other in numerous ways in addition to their levels of introversion and extraversion or neuroticism. One particularly obvious difference among people is their level of intelligence, and there are various reasons for arguing that clever people might tend to be happier than dull ones. The most important reason is that intelligence is a highly valued resource in society. Children of high intelligence are more successful at school, pass more examinations, and subsequently move on to more interesting, respected, and well-paid careers than those of lower intelligence.

Despite the fact that it definitely seems preferable to be clever rather than dull, there is very little evidence that intelligence is related in any way to happiness. What is going on here? Some cynics have suggested that those of low intelligence are relatively happy because they do not understand the full horrors and dangers of contemporary society. However, this view is not supported by any real evidence.

It is much more fruitful to focus on the role played by individual differences in the desire for achievement and in aspiration levels. Those of high intelligence often believe that their intellectual abilities should open up interesting career opportunities, and so set themselves rather high levels of aspiration. If they are unsuccessful in living up to these high aspirations, then this can be a recipe for unhappiness. In contrast, less intelligent people are more likely to set themselves relatively modest career goals, which may well be achievable and thus a source of happiness.

COMMON SENSE?

One of the problems which psychologists are always battling with is that when people are provided with the answer to a psychological puzzle, they tend to argue that it is rather obvious. There is a danger that this fate may befall the notion that personality is the most important single factor in influencing an individual's level of happiness. Before defending the non-obviousness of the argument developed in this chapter, I would like to dwell briefly on the phenomenon of being wise after the event. A case in point concerns the famous or notorious research carried out some years ago by Stanley Milgram. He discovered that the number of people prepared to administer potentially lethal 450-volt electric shocks to an innocent victim when commanded to do so by a psychologist was approximately 500 times greater than most people guessed it would be. However, when people were told that almost two-thirds of Milgram's subjects were willing to give massive electric shocks, they expressed little surprise, and quickly explained away the findings in terms of obedience to authority.

The tendency to be wise after the event and to concoct plausible explanations for the unexpected can sometimes be rather amusing. Students who failed to solve a difficult reasoning problem were provided with solutions, and asked to justify them. Nearly all of the students came up with lengthy justifications of the solution they had been given. What gives this experiment its point is that the students were given a variety of different solutions, all of which were incorrect!

Let us return to the matter of the involvement of personality in human happiness. It is a fact that when people are asked about the factors responsible for happiness they typically refer to good health, financial security, satisfactory family life, an interesting job, and so on, but very rarely do they mention personality. On those occasions when someone has asked you why you are happy, I am very confident that you did not reply, "Because I am a stable extravert!" To take another example, when we compare our lives with those led by our friends and acquaintances, we perhaps feel that the Smiths are happier than us because they have a new baby, or more money than us, or a new

Volvo estate car, whereas the Jones family are less happy because Mr. Jones is worried that he may become redundant. It is undeniable that many experiences do affect our enjoyment of life, and some may have a devastating effect on us. Nevertheless, our personality will exert a much stronger and longer-lasting influence on our normal level of happiness than the specific experiences we have from day to day. Of course, when we are trying to explain why someone is very happy, it is easy to seize on a new baby or a new house as the reason. However, what we need to do is to move beyond such concrete events and consider something more abstract that has a pervasive influence on emotinal moods: the rich pattern of human personality.

PERSONALITY AND HAPPINESS

The notion that happiness depends in a major way on personality can be tested in ways other than those already discussed. For example, Paul Costa and Robert McCrae argued that an individual's personality as assessed at one point in time ought to predict reasonably well how happy that person would be several years later. They investigated what happened over an interval of 10 years. Their prediction was convincingly supported, in spite of the fact that they took no account at all of each individual's experiences during those 10 years!

If some people possess the "happiness gene" whereas other possess the "unhappiness gene", then it follows that most people should be either reasonably happy or unhappy with all of the major areas of life. Thus, someone who is happily married should tend to be happy in his or her work, happy with his or her friends, and so on. If, on the other hand, happiness depended purely on the specific experiences which occur in each area of life, there would be no reason why happiness at work or at home should be associated with happiness in the rest of life. In fact, it seems very strongly to be the case that people are either reasonably happy or unhappy in general, and happiness levels for any particular individual do not usually vary much across the different areas of life.

There are a number of ways of trying to make sense of the fact that there are substantial individual differences in the ability to derive happiness from life's experiences. In general terms, naturally happy individuals appear to view the world through rose-coloured spectacles, so that everything is seen in a somewhat more positive and optimistic manner than is the case for other people. Of course, they become upset and worried when major problems or misfortunes occur, but they do not permit these calamities to overwhelm them in the way that others might. In contrast, neurotic introverts tend to put an unduly negative and pessimistic interpretation on life's events; this might be described as viewing the world through blue-coloured spectacles. For them, a minor failure is interpreted as profoundly symbolic of their general inadequacy. Success and pleasurable events do produce happiness for neurotic introverts, but that happiness is regarded as transitory and undeserved. Thus, individual differences in personality lead us to colour the world with characteristic kinds of interpretation that are either predominantly positive or negative in nature. It is these permanent individual differences which make our world a heaven or a hell.

While personality affects happiness directly by influencing the emotional reaction to life's events, it also has other, more subtle, effects. For example, an individual's life-style reflects to some extent his or her personality. If we know that individual A prefers to live alone, likes to read a lot, does not want to have many friends, and likes to be a loner, whereas individual B loves parties, has numerous friends, and likes to socialize nearly every evening, then we can be fairly confident that individual B is considerably more extraverted than individual A. Thus, we are what we like, and the life-style favoured by extraverts is more conducive to positive affect than is the life-style of introverts.

The idea that personality can be inferred with some accuracy from the activities he or she chooses to engage in receives considerable support when we compare the more adventurous and sociable life-style of the typical extravert with the quieter and more restricted life-style of the introvert. However, what is surprising is that the link between personality and life-style is often rather weak or even non-existent. Extraverts and introverts do differ in their life-styles, but the leading British psychologist Adrian Furnham has discovered that people who are high or low in neuroticism hardly differ in terms of their activity patterns or the leisure pursuits they prefer.

Why should this be so? One of the reasons for assuming that personality predicts life-style is that people presumably spend more time in those situations likely to produce happy emotions than in those situations producing less happy experiences. However, what we do with our time is determined by our responsibilities and commitments as well as by our search for happiness. Those high and low in neuroticism differ in their susceptibility to negative affect, so that one might imagine that neurotic individuals would try to steer clear of situations which might produce negative affect. However, there are problems with this strategy, because many of the situations which may lead to substantial negative affect (e.g., social situations; competitive situations) can also be associated with powerful positive affect.

Recent work by Ed Diener, mentioned briefly earlier in the chapter, has provided further insights into why it is that introverts and extraverts differ in their life-style but neurotics and stables do not. A crucial question which he asked was whether experiences of positive and negative affect depend more on the individual person or on the situations he or she happens to be in. For negative affect, the influence of the individual was NINE times greater than that of the situation! In other words, some individuals have high negative affect virtually regardless of the situation they are in, whereas others have low negative affect across most situations. For positive affect, the person had only twice as much impact as the situation. Thus, positive affect varies greatly from one person to the next, but it also depends to a fair extent on the situation you are in.

These findings provide some of the strongest evidence that happiness (and its two major components positive and negative affect) is determined much more by personality than by the situation. This is especially true of negative affect, with those high in neuroticism being generally high in negative affect and those low in neuroticism being low in negative affect. There is little reason for the two groups to adopt different life-styles, because the influence of the situation on negative affect is so modest.

In contrast, the amount of positive affect we experience is much affected by the situation we are in, and this is particularly true for extraverts. As a consequence, extraverts know the kinds of stimulating and social situations that will tend to increase their positive affect, and therefore put themselves in those situations. Introverts, on the other hand, have less capacity for experiencing positive affect, and so have little incentive to emulate the very active life-style of the extravert.

There may be important practical implications of these findings. If you want to make yourself happier, you can focus on reducing negative affect or on increasing positive affect. Since positive affect is more readily altered than negative affect by moving from one situation to another, it follows that it is usually quicker and easier to boost positive affect than to reduce negative affect.

NATIONAL DIFFERENCES

Stereotypes

Many people who travel frequently to other countries have a distinct impression that the inhabitants of different lands vary greatly in their personality and their enjoyment of life. Of course, such impressions are often clouded by prejudice and suspicion. Throughout virtually the whole of recorded human history, people have been comparing the group or groups to which they belong with other groups. Whatever groups have been compared, the almost invariant rule is for one's own group to show up favourably in the comparison.

For a variety of reasons which are often obscured by the mists of time, people who belong to one country typically make a habit of picking on the members of just one foreign country for particular attack. So far as the English are concerned, they have tended to single out the Irish, although the Scots, Welsh, French, and Germans have also received their fair share of scorn and contempt. For the benefit of non-English readers, the English have emphasized the alleged stupidity of the Irish, as exemplified in the following "witticism": When Paddy discovered his wife was going to have triplets, he was puzzled. "Who were the other two men?" he asked.

In very much the same way that the English belittle the Irish, the French speak in a disparaging way of the Belgians, and the Flemings take their spleen out on the Walloons. However, as the Englishman Alan Coren demonstrated amusingly, there is no reason at all why we should restrict our barbed comments to just one other nationality. He pointed out that France "is the largest country in Europe, a great boon for drunks, who need room to fall . . . The houses are all shuttered to exclude light, as a precaution against hangovers, and filled with large lumpy beds in which the French spend 83.7 per cent of their time recovering from sex or booze or both. The lumpiness is due, of course, to the presence of undeclared income under the mattresses."

Coren then turned his critical eye on the inhabitants of Italy: "The median Italian . . . is a cowardly baritone who consumes 78.3 kilogrammes of carbohydrates a month and drives about in a car slightly smaller than he is, looking for a divorce."

In general terms, many English people regard the inhabitants of northern European countries as relatively dour and unhappy. This is thought to be especially true of the Scandinavians, who allegedly spend the long, dark, winter nights either contemplating or committing suicide. On the other hand, the Mediterranean types such as the Italians and the Spanish are regarded as somewhat hysterical and over-emotional.

Of course, many national stereotypes are totally inaccurate and merely based on ignorance and prejudice. The stereotype which Americans have of the English is of a tradition-loving, reserved, sophisticated, intelligent, and conventional people, but we can all think of numerous English people who are almost the opposite of this stereotype. When Americans are asked to describe the typical American, they describe him (or her) as being materialistic, intelligent, industrious, pleasure-loving, and individualistic. Once again, this stereotype scarcely fits millions of Americans.

The Facts

Despite the fact that national stereotypes are often affected by prejudice and over-simplification, there are still many people (including myself) who remain obstinately convinced that there are genuine differences among nationalities. A personal anecdote may help to show why I hold this rather unfashionable view. A few years ago, we had a summer holiday in Switzerland and Italy. Our daughter, Fleur, was only two years old at the time, and I remember vividly the markedly different reactions to her shown by the Swiss and the Italians. In Switzerland, she was totally ignored in shops, cafés, and restaurants. In Italy, on the other hand, countless total strangers went out of their way to admire her and to remark on her beauty. At one restaurant, the waitress was so taken by Fleur that she insisted on the chef coming out of the kitchen to have a look at her!

The fact that people within any one country span the whole range of personality from extreme extravert to extreme introvert, and from highly neurotic to very stable might seem to invalidate the attempt to uncover national differences. This is an erroneous view. When we talk about national differences, we are focussing on what is true on average in each country. Thus, for example, even though many Americans are introverted and many English people are extraverted, it is still entirely possible that the average American is more extraverted than the average English person.

Fortunately, there is a reasonable amount of evidence available which can be used to resolve the controversy over the validity of national stereotypes. Richard Lynn of the New University of Ulster pioneered a rather ingenious way of proceeding, which involves determining whether the inhabitants of different countries vary in their characteristic levels of anxiety and extraversion. He claimed that one can make use of national differences in the prevalence of mental illness, accidents, murder, divorce, alcoholism, and so on. With respect to neuroticism or anxiety, the argument was that, just as individuals who have accidents, become alcoholic, or commit suicide tend to have anxious or neurotic personalities, so countries with a high incidence of accidents, alcoholism, and suicide have relatively anxious populations. Since extraverted individuals are known to be more likely than introverts to have accidents, to smoke cigarettes, to have illegitimate children, and to commit murder, national differences in all of these factors may reflect the extent to which the members of a country tend to be extraverted or introverted.

When Richard Lynn collected the relevant data for the 18 economically advanced nations of northern Europe, North America, and Australasia, it was Austria that emerged as the most anxious nation, followed by Japan, France, Germany, and Italy. At the other extreme, the much maligned Irish emerged as easily the least anxious nation, with the United Kingdom, New Zealand, and the Netherlands also being low in anxiety. On the extraversion dimension, the Americans conformed to their stereotype by being the most extraverted nation, followed by Finland, Austria, and Sweden (!). At the other end of the scale, the most introverted countries were Japan, the Netherlands, and Norway.

We can use these findings to identify in a provisional way the fun countries where happiness is the norm. The basic strategy is the same as that used to locate happy individuals: what we are looking for is a combination of high positive affect (in the form of extraversion) and low negative affect (in the form of stability or low neuroticism or anxiety). On that basis, the country with the happiest population is the United States of America, followed in order by Sweden, the United Kingdom, and Ireland. However, the precise way in which happiness is achieved varies from country to country. Thus, Americans appear to be a happy people largely because of the high positive affect stemming from their extraversion rather than because of their low negative affect. In contrast, the British and the Irish achieve happiness by being very stable, non-neurotic, and low in negative affect, rather than via bubbling enthusiasm and zest.

Intriguing additional information about the high level of happiness enjoyed by the British has recently been provided by Gallup's Social Surveys Department. Gordon Heald, who works for Gallup, explained what really excites the British: "For thousands of them happiness consists of an all-family video session while eating an Indian or Chinese takeaway."

The most morose or unhappy countries are those which have the unfortunate combination of introversion (which produces low positive affect) and high neuroticism or anxiety (which produces high negative affect). The Japanese emerge from this analysis as the clear winners in the unhappiness stakes, followed in the rank order by France, Italy, and West Germany. The Japanese were the only nation to show very high introversion and very high neuroticism or anxiety, with the other unhappy countries falling into that category primarily because of high neuroticism or anxiety rather than high introversion.

These findings are mostly rather comforting to members of the English-speaking world, who for that reason may feel inclined to take them at face value. However, it is perfectly reasonable to argue that national rates of murder, alcoholism, and so on are all very interesting, but that it is far-fetched to attempt to assess the general level of happiness in a country on the basis of the extreme minority who become murderers, alcoholics, or who commit suicide. It is generally accepted that there is some truth in this argument, and as a result psychologists in several different countries have measured personality on an individual basis by means of standardized questionnaires. The results of such questionnaire studies have proved to be reassuringly close to those that Richard Lynn obtained with his demographic variables.

Why do nations differ in happiness?

A vexed question when considering the differences in happiness level from one country to another is to explain where these differences have come from. Since happiness depends on personality, it is tempting to propose that significant differences in genetic make-up from country to country account for the variation in national happiness levels. There is at present very little evidence on this matter, but there are one or two straws in the wind. For example, it has been found that introversion in Europeans is associated with the AB blood group, and the introverted Japanese have three times as many people with that blood group as the British.

Another theory that might help to explain some of the national differences is based on the notion of selective emigration. Perhaps the more extraverted members of a population seek the excitement and risk involved in uprooting oneself and one's family in order to live abroad. The simplest way to test this theory is to compare new nations whose populations are almost entirely made up of relatively recent immigrants (e.g., the United States of America, Canada, and Australia) against the nations of northwest Europe from which the majority of the immigrants came. The new nations are definitely more extraverted (and thus higher in positive affect) than the countries of northwest Europe, and so selective emigration may be playing a part. However, selective emigration fails to account for national differences in neuroticism or anxiety, and so it cannot provide a complete explanation of national happiness levels.

A more promising explanation of national differences in happiness starts from the fact that mood is influenced by climatic conditions. Who has not had the experience of an uplift in mood upon discovering that the day will be sunny and warm or of sinking spirits on looking out on a scene of black clouds and driving rain? Numerous aspects of the weather seem to be related to mood, ranging from humidity to temperature, and from barometric pressure to hours of sunshine. It is well-known, for example, that many people suffer from a form of depression known as seasonal affective disorder. It usually strikes during the winter months when the days are short and there is little light. Under these circumstances, the pineal gland in the brain produces more of a hormone called melatonin, which in turn causes depression. The more favourable climatic conditions of spring reduce the manufacture of melatonin and help to create "spring fever".

A promising contender for a climatic variable that affects happiness directly is heat or temperature. People exposed to extreme heat become more aggressive and more willing to administer electric shocks to another person. This is entirely in line with our frequent use of heat- and fire-related imagery to describe angry and aggressive states, including expressions such as "being hot under the collar" and "doing a slow burn".

The link between extreme heat and aggression was confirmed in an analysis of approximately 100 violent riots that occurred in the United States of America between 1967 and 1971. When the temperature was above 90° Fahrenheit, a riot was five times more likely to occur than when the temperature was in the low 60s. As usual, that great intuitive psychologist William Shakespeare managed to express an important psychological truth in elegant form:

> The day is hot, the Capulets abroad,
> And if we meet we shall not scape a brawl;
> For now, these hot days, is the mad blood stirring.
> (*Romeo and Juliet*)

Temperature has been found to have quite a marked effect on a number of measures related to anxiety as well as anger. Thus, most suicides occur in the spring or summer, and juvenile sexual offences are most prevalent in the summer months. Cases of mania, which involve a very high level of excitability and general physiological arousal, are almost twice as frequent during the early summer as in the depths of winter.

From these findings, it might be expected that countries exposed to great summer heat should have anxious and unhappy populations as a result, whereas more temperate climates may characterize the stable or happy countries. Japan is the advanced country with the unhappiest population, and intriguingly it also on average has the hottest summers. The other countries that are relatively unhappy are Italy, France, and West Germany. Italy has the second hottest summers of the 18 countries considered by Richard Lynn, and France comes fifth on the list. However, the theory applies less well to West Germany, which does not tend to have very hot summers.

The countries with the most contented or happy inhabitants are Ireland, the United Kingdom, Sweden, and the United States of America. Precisely in line with expectation, Ireland has the coolest summers of any of the 18 countries, followed closely by the United Kingdom and Sweden. The United States does not fit the picture, however, because it has quite hot summers.

Overall, then, the climatic theory of national happiness levels seems to fit the facts reasonably well. Three-quarters of the unhappiest countries have particularly hot summers, and three-quarters of the happiest countries experience very cool summers. It would be ludicrous to ignore other determinants of national happiness such as racial tensions, political stability or instability, affluence or poverty, but it is very likely that the weather is a contributory factor. It is interesting in this connection to note that many people have divided Western Europe into the Southern European or Mediterranean type on the one hand, and the Northern European or Nordic type on the other. The main difference that has been suggested between them is that the Mediterranean type is hot-blooded and over-emotional, whereas the Nordic type is seen as more reserved and calmer (which may be true) and also as less happy (which is not true). What is noteworthy is that the commonsensical distinction closely parallels a climatic one, since the weather tends to be hotter in the Mediterranean countries than in the north of Europe. As we have seen, it is climate which holds the key to national differences in happiness.

CHAPTER THREE

The Pleasures of Sex

Many of our most euphoric and thrilling experiences occur in a sexual context, and it would be unduly puritanical to deny it. When people are asked which leisure-time pursuit they enjoy most, the clear winner up until later middle age is sexual activity. In one study, approximately 2000 British men and women were asked to agree or disagree with the statement "Sex is far and away my greatest pleasure." Thirty-five per cent of the men and 26 per cent of the women agreed with the statement. Given these facts, it is clearly essential for a book on happiness to consider the part played by sexual activity in promoting happiness. It is also important to consider whether men and women differ in their enjoyment of sexual activity, since many have claimed that there are substantial differences between them.

Of course, sexual activity can produce pain and unhappiness as well as pleasure and happiness. Sometimes the problems are mainly of a physical nature. When a premature ejaculator attempts sexual intercourse with an unresponsive and frigid woman, the effect resembles what happens if you try to push a marshmallow into a coin slot. At other times, the problems are psychological, with sex leaving the participants feeling guilty, anxious, and embarrassed. Sex in a loving context is usually much more pleasurable than in its absence, but some may agree with Woody Allen's remark that "Sex without love is one of my favourite meaningless activities." In spite of all of the potential problems and disappointments that sex can involve, the contemplation of, and indulgence in, sexual activity occupies a substantial amount of time in most people's lives.

One of the most intriguing questions in this area of life is whether there are major differences between men and women in terms of the happiness and fulfilment they derive from sexual activity. A view that enjoys some popularity is that men are much more interested than women in sex, and that they find it more enjoyable than women. This point of view was more common many years ago than it is now. In the Victorian era, for example, girls who were about to be married were told that they should lie still and think of England while various nasty and unspeakable things were done to them.

SOCIOBIOLOGY

Nowadays we tend to regard Victorian morality as being rather laughable. However, the notion that the sexes differ enormously in their attitudes to sex has been given an apparently scientific underpinning in modern times by the sociobiologists. Much to the fury and indignation of feminists everywhere, sociobiologists claim that natural selection favours men who help to ensure the survival of the species by having sex with numerous women, whereas women need to be much more careful because they have the long and arduous task of caring for any offspring that result. The idea that men who are promiscuous are to be congratulated for ensuring the survival of the human race seems worthy of inclusion in Hugh Hefner's "playboy philosophy", but may not appeal to many other people.

Despite the apparent implausibility of the sociobiologists' position, there are some facts which fit it. It seems to follow from their viewpoint that the great majority of human societies should be polygamous, i.e., some men having more than one wife, and that is what actually happens. Moreover, the sociobiologists have a ready answer to the vexed question of why it is that men often reach orgasm before women during sexual intercourse. Laurence Hong of California State University, Los Angeles, argued that rapid orgasm and ejaculation on the man's part used to be very advantageous in the past, because it enabled him to deposit his semen inside the female before he could be stopped by other males or by wild animals.

The average American man can achieve orgasm in a little under two minutes, and Laurence Hong wondered whether this was quicker than other species. It turns out that the American man does quite badly in the speed stakes. The chimpanzee races to orgasm in just seven seconds, the lemur in under 10 seconds, and the gibbon in 15 seconds. Of the great apes, only the orang-utan exceeds man in ejaculatory control, taking a remarkably leisurely and self-indulgent 10.8 minutes. Sociobiologists conclude from these findings that nature wants male primates to reach orgasm with the minimum of delay. Of course, the orang-utan is an exception to the rule, so how can his dilatoriness be accounted for? One theory is that the orang-utan can afford to take his time because he is highly aggressive, and is thus able to keep trouble at bay during his 11-minute exertions.

Few women are likely to be terribly enthusiastic about the notion that premature ejaculation by men is actually a good thing and in excellent accord with the laws of nature. Where, I hear my female readers ask, does the female orgasm fit into the sociobiologists' scheme of things? The short answer is that it receives scant attention, perhaps because the overwhelming majority of sociobiologists are men. The general idea put forward by sociobiologists is that the female orgasm is totally irrelevant to reproduction and the continuation of the species, and thus is of little theoretical interest. This disinclination to consider the female orgasm in detail is rather like King Canute trying to stop the tide coming in. In recent years there has been intense discussion by doctors, sexologists, and marriage counsellors about the importance of the female orgasm, and how to ensure that it happens. However, sociobiologists point out that this concern is of relatively recent origin, and limited primarily to the Western world. It is still the norm in most human societies for the man to proceed rapidly and vigorously to orgasm without bothering very much about the satisfaction (or otherwise) of his female partner.

The sweeping conclusions about the sexual natures of men and women to which sociobiologists feel inexorably drawn were expressed in the following ringing tones by Donald Symons: "With respect to sexuality, there is a female human nature and a male human nature, and these natures are extraordinarily different . . . Men and women differ in their sexual natures because throughout the immensely long hunting and gathering phase of human evolutionary history the sexual desires and dispositions that were adaptive for either sex, were for the other, tickets to reproductive oblivion."

Sociobiologists have tended to base their explanations of human sexuality on the assumptions that men are naturally more promiscuous than women, and that men have a greater sex drive or libido. These "facts" are increasingly being disputed, and it is of interest to note that views about female sexuality have altered dramatically over the centuries. If we go back to the writings of the ancient Romans and Greeks, we discover numerous complaints about the excessive sexuality displayed by women. In the 15th century, it was often claimed that women's extreme sexuality made them receptive to the devil, which led to them turning into witches.

It was only comparatively recently that any proper factual data about male and female sexuality have become available. The pioneer was the remarkable scientist Alfred Kinsey, who began publishing his epoch-making reports on sexuality in the 1940s. He discovered that the average red-blooded American man had notched up a grand total of 1,523 orgasms before he got married, whereas the average American girl was lagging far behind with only 223 orgasms. This sevenfold difference may appear to confirm the greater sexuality of the male, but more recent evidence shows conclusively that the "orgasm gap" is closing fast. Our rapid perusal of history suggests that most of the allegedly greater sex drive of the male is actually due to social conditioning along the lines of "Nice girls don't", and that there are no major biological differences in libido or sex drive between the sexes. However, there may be one important exception to that generalization. Men reach the peak of their physical sexual capacity while still in their teens, while women reach theirs only some ten years later. As a consequence, it is quite likely that young men are more highly sexed than young women, but the opposite may well be the norm a few years later.

SEXUAL SATISFACTION

Men and women differ relatively little in terms of sex drive or libido, and the same appears to be true of the pleasure or satisfaction derived from different sexual activities. A particularly thorough investigation of sexual pleasure in men and women was carried out by Caroline Waterman and Emil Chiauzzi. They used as their sample 42 young couples attending a large northeastern state university in the United States of America. The questions they asked ranged over numerous sexual activities, including male manual manipulation of the female genitals, female manual manipulation of the male genitals, male oral stimulation of the female genitals (technically known as "cunnilingus"), female oral stimulation of the male genitals (known as "fellatio"), and sexual intercourse. All of these activities were rated for pleasure when they occurred with and without orgasm.

The most striking and clearcut finding was that the pleasure ratings were remarkably similar for men and women. In general, both sexes preferred each sexual activity when it was NOT accompanied by orgasm. This seems strange in view of the considerable pleasure usually associated with orgasm, but most people prefer to "save" their orgasm for sexual intercourse. Such sex differences as were discovered indicated a somewhat selfish preference for activities centred on oneself rather than one's partner. Thus, women obtained more pleasure than men from cunnilingus and from having their partner handle their genitals, and men gave higher pleasure ratings than women to fellatio and to having their partner handle their genitals. Of all the sexual activities rated for pleasure, there was only one where there was a substantial difference between men and women. That was fellatio to orgasm, where the enthusiasm of the men was quite unmatched by that of the women. This may explain why this specific sexual activity is much requested by men who go to prostitutes.

For better or worse, most discussion of the happiness and joy produced by sexual activity has focussed on orgasm or the big "O". This is in spite of the fact that (as we have just seen) much of the pleasure derived from sexual activity does not stem directly from orgasm. Not surprisingly, women tend to prefer sexual intercourse when it produces orgasm than when it does not, but many women report that the most pleasurable physical sensation occurring during intercourse is the moment at which the penis penetrates the vagina. With these qualifications in mind, let us turn to the male and female orgasms in the context of human sexual activity.

There is far more similarity between men and women at the physiological level than meets the eye. Initially, all normal human embryos are potentially bisexual. The penis and the clitoris develop out of the same tissue, as do the scrotum and the labia majora, the penile urethral tube and the labia minora, and the testes and the ovaries. The clitoris is much smaller than the penis, but it nevertheless contains approximately the same number of nerve endings.

William Masters and Virginia Johnson studied human sexual response in detail, and identified a basic four-stage sequence in both sexes. The first stage of excitement is followed by a plateau, then orgasm, and finally resolution. The plateau phase is a short-lasting period of intense anticipatory tension, which serves as the launching pad for the peak of orgasmic release. Heart rate rises during the excitement phase, and then levels off at 120–130 beats per minute during the plateau phase, before increasing to 160–170 beats per minute at orgasm, and then returning to normal during the resolution phase. During the pre-orgasmic stages, the nipples of the breasts become erect in almost all women, and erection of the nipples also occurs in approximately 30 per cent of men. The reddish sex flush develops during the plateau phase; it sometimes extends to the face, throat, shoulders, breasts, and abdomen, and terminates with the onset of orgasm.

Orgasm itself has dramatic effects in both sexes. The breathing rate doubles or even trebles, there are contractions of the anal sphincter, the face screws up in apparent agony, and there is a sudden release of tension. Muscular spasms sometimes occur in the hands and feet, in the long muscles of the arms, necks, and legs, and in the muscles of the lower back and buttocks. Thus, orgasm is properly regarded as a response of the entire body rather than just of the genitals. The similarity between the male and female orgasms even extends to the interval between successive orgasmic contractions, which is about four-fifths of a second in both sexes. A minor difference, however, is that women have more orgasmic contractions than men. In addition, men tend to experience the initial contractions as most intense and the subsequent ones as weaker, whereas the opposite is true of women.

ORGASM AND EJACULATION

It has nearly always been assumed that there is at least one very significant difference between the male and female orgasms, namely, that orgasm must be accompanied by ejaculation in the male, but that ejaculation never happens in the female. These assumptions may be universally accepted, but they are both false.

Mina Robbins and Gordon Jensen provided the first systematic evidence that orgasm and ejaculation can occur separately from each other in the male. They asked for men who claimed to experience orgasm without ejaculation to step forward in the name of science, and managed to establish contact with 13 such men. All of them claimed that they had somewhere betweeen three and ten orgasms during intercourse before they finally ejaculated. Since men throughout the ages have boasted untruthfully of their sexual prowess, Robbins and Jensen decided to test the men's multiple orgasmic responses by physiological monitoring using a polygraph. They discovered that these men did, indeed, have orgasms without ejaculation, and these orgasms were remarkably similar to normal orgasms with ejaculation.

The notion that women can ejaculate during orgasm makes some sense if we consider the physiological similarities between men and women. However, the famous sex researchers William Masters and Virginia Johnson concluded after detailed physiological examination of the female sexual apparatus that the idea of female ejaculation is an "erroneous but widespread concept." Despite their expert opinion, more recent evidence leaves no doubt that at least some women can ejaculate. It is also quite clear that female ejaculation is triggered off by stimulation of the so-called "Grafenberg spot", which can be felt through the upper wall of the vagina near the entrance. As is the case with men, the female ejaculate and urine are delivered through the same tube, namely the urethra.

One of the peculiarities of the female ejaculate is the sheer volume of liquid produced. The volume of a single male ejaculation varies between about 0.2 and 6.6 millilitres, with 13 millilitres being the highest ever recorded (is this an all-comers' record?). In contrast, the volume of the female ejaculate is of the order of 10 to 25 millilitres.

All in all, the physiological evidence indicates very strongly that male and female orgasms are strikingly alike. Alfred Kinsey concluded from researches that the only phenomenon in the entire physiology of sexual response which was not closely similar in men and women was ejaculation. However, we have just seen that female ejaculation is alive and well, differing from male ejaculation primarily in its frequency of occurrence. To the extent that the pleasure and happiness derived from sexual activity depends on physiological responses, the natural expectation is that men and women would find sex comparably enjoyable.

FIRST EXPERIENCE

Of course, there is often a large gap between the physiological and the psychological. Perhaps women find sex less pleasurable than men because of lingering remnants of Victorian morality, which suggested that well-bred young ladies should not enjoy sexual activity. If this old-fashioned morality continues to exist at all, it would presumably affect a girl's first experience of sex. This was explored by David Weis. The average age of the girls was 16, and their partner was typically 2.5 years older. First intercourse occurred in many different settings, but for 75 per cent of the girls it was a private home. Thirty-eight per cent of the girls felt guilty, and 31 per cent felt embarrassed, but the most common reported emotions were nervousness, excitement, fear, romance, tension, and pleasure.

These emotional reactions are not very different to those of boys losing their virginity, except that boys are much less likely to feel guilty. Thus, enjoyment of the first sexual intercourse may be lower in girls than in boys because of moral doctrines. However,while conventional morality would regard the nature of the relationship as making a difference, the girls actually enjoyed the experience as much with someone they had just met as with their fiancé). What did matter was whether or not the lover was gentle, loving, and considerate, and familiar settings were associated with more pleasure than a motel or hotel bedroom.

THE ORGASM

The first sexual experience is obviously special and noteworthy, and may not be very indicative of how much pleasure and happiness are normally obtained from sexual activity. However, it seems on the face of it rather difficult to compare the emotional and other psychological reactions of men and women to sexual experiences. How can a man possibly know just what it is like for a woman to experience an orgasm, for example, or vice versa? There may be no perfectly satisfactory answer, but a good start was made by Ellen Vance and Nathaniel Wagner. They asked college students to write descriptions of how they felt when they were having an orgasm. Not surprisingly, they confirmed that orgasms are generally regarded as extremely pleasurable, happiness-inducing experiences. One student described the experience as follows: "The feeling of orgasm in my opinion is a feeling of utmost relief of any type of tension. It is the most fulfilling experience I have ever had of enjoyment. The feeling is exuberant and the most enjoyable feeling I have ever experienced." Another student described the orgasmic experience as follows: "An orgasm feels like heaven in the heat of hell; a tremendous build-up within of pleasure that makes the tremendous work of releasing that pleasure worthwhile."

If we are interested in trying to decide whether male and female experiences of orgasm are basically the same, then we can make use of these descriptions. One of the above descriptions was written by a man and the other by a woman. Can you work out which is which? In fact, the first one was written by a woman and the second one by a man. If you were right about these two descriptions, then try to decide about the following two accounts of the orgasmic experience: "Has a build-up in the genitals with involuntary thrusting of hips and twitching of thigh muscles. Also contracting and releasing of the genital muscles. The pressure becomes quite intense—like there is something underneath the skin of the genitals pushing out. Then there is a sudden release of the tension with contraction of genitals with a feeling of release and relaxation." Here is the second account: "A feeling of intense physical and mental satisfaction. The height of a sexual encounter. Words can hardly describe a feeling so great."

Both of the above descriptions were written by young women. Ellen Vance and Nathaniel Wagner collected these descriptions (and several others). Then they presented them to various groups of people, including expert gynaecologists and psychologists, who were asked to pick out those written by men and by women. These professional experts showed a marked lack of ability to do this at better than chance level. Thus, the subjective experience of orgasm is very similar for men and women.

Some female readers may be puzzled at this point. Ellen Vance and Nathaniel talked about the female orgasm, but many women are adamant that orgasms produced in different ways lead to distinctly different feelings. The notion that all forms of female orgasm are very similar receives some support from the pioneering work of Masters and Johnson in the 1960s. They claimed that the female orgasm always involves the same physiological processes irrespective of the circumstances. Mind you, the fact that the women were studied under laboratory conditions while wired up to physiological recording instruments may have distorted the findings. It is certainly true that most female orgasms are produced through direct or indirect stimulation of the clitoris, but the recent discovery of the Grafenberg spot means that we must abandon the notion of THE female orgasm. This may be less true of male orgasms. It has been suggested that the male orgasm is a rose-is-a-rose-is-a-rose thing, whereas the female orgasm ranges all the way from poppies to orchids.

When women are asked to indicate what their orgasms in various circumstances are like, they usually describe orgasms that happen while masturbating in rather different terms to those occurring during sexual intercourse. Masturbatory orgasms are typically very intense but of short duration. They are usually experienced on the surface of the vagina, and often fail to provide a feeling of release. In contrast, orgasms during intercourse last much longer, do not reach an intense peak, are experienced internally, and are followed by a profound feeling of satisfaction and release.

A related distinction is that between clitoral and vaginal orgasms. Naturally enough, Sigmund Freud, the grandfather of sex research, had his own theory about this. Initially a little girl is mainly attached to her mother, whom she treats as a love object. However, she imagines that she once possessed a penis but lost it through castration, and she blames her mother for its loss. She is also angry at her mother for forbidding masturbation, and so she turns to her father as love object. Accompanying this shift from the mother to the father is clitoral-vaginal transfer, in which the girl's interest moves from her clitoris to her vagina. Within this theoretical framework, clitoral sex is relatively immature and "bad", whereas vaginal sex is the "normal" and mature pattern.

Seymour Fisher found that young married women reported that clitoral and vaginal stimulation produced different subjective feelings. These differences were expressed very articulately by one of them: "Clitoral stimulation has a high intensity—feelings concentrated in one spot. It's a lightness, a spark, almost ticklish sensation. I feel sort of an electricity. I feel the pleasure is all physical. In a vaginal stimulation the pleasure is mental or spiritual, a feeling of depth or meaning. A wider area of pleasurable sensation. It produces a longing or hunger. It is a comforting pleasure. Vaginal stimulation is like a warm bath of pleasure. My whole body responds to vaginal stimulation; and it moves and it feels. In clitoral stimulation my body is rigid with expectation of continuing pleasure. Vaginal stimulation is like a hum but clitoral is a high-pitched note. From clitoral stimulation my body demands to be satisfied, from vaginal my body is content even if it's not."

The above account comes from a young woman who obtains much gratification from both clitoral and vaginal stimulation. However, many women have clear preferences about the kind of stimulation they enjoy. Seymour Fisher had the gall to ask 500 married women "If you had the choice of receiving only clitoral or vaginal stimulation, which would you prefer?" The clear winner was clitoral stimulation, which was chosen by nearly two-thirds of the women, against under one-third who opted for vaginal stimulation. The clitoral and vaginal women did not differ in their reported frequency of orgasm, the frequency of sexual intercourse, the average length of foreplay, or the number of different positions used in intercourse. However, those who preferred clitoral stimulation were more likely to regard their orgasms as ecstatic, whereas those who chose vaginal stimulation tended to describe their orgasms as happy. There were some interesting differences between the two types of women. Vaginal women were more inclined to assert that their bodies were like non-living objects, and that they were relatively unaware of, and distant from, their bodies. Vaginal women were also more likely to say that they had experienced a psychological disturbance, and they were rated as being more anxious and tense than clitoral women. Most of these findings are in the opposite direction to that predicted by Sigmund Freud, who claimed that vaginal sex is somehow superior and preferable.

ORAL SEX

The approach taken by Seymour Fisher is limited in that he hardly mentions fellatio and cunnilingus, which are increasingly common forms of sexual activity. This is perhaps especially true of young unmarried people. There has been much publicity in the media about the substantial increase in sexual activity among the young, but what has gone relatively unnoticed is a shift in the kinds of sexual activity engaged in. Young people used to experience normal intercourse earlier in time than oral sex, but nowadays the sequence is often reversed. Edward Herold and Leslie Way compared the incidence of intercourse and of oral sex among young single females at a university in Ontario, Canada. Considering only those who had not had intercourse, 20 per cent had performed fellatio on their male partner, and 35 per cent had experienced cunnilingus. In contrast, virtually all of those who had had intercourse had also performed and received oral sex.

Why are many young people willing to engage in oral sex but reluctant to have intercouse? One factor is religiosity or the intensity of religious beliefs. Teenagers who do not have any strong religious convictions tend to experience intercourse before oral sex, but the opposite is true of the highly religious. Religious values have traditionally condemned intercourse and the loss of virginity before marriage, and so oral sex can apparently be an ingenious way of reconciling sexual desires with the teachings of the Church. However, what these teenagers conveniently forget is that many religions also condemn oral sex.

How does oral sex compare to other forms of sexual activity in its ability to produce happiness and enjoyment? While the differences are not large, men tend to report that sexual intercourse is more pleasurable than fellatio, and women prefer intercourse to cunnilingus. If we include manual manipulation of the genitals, then men enjoy that less than either fellatio or intercourse. Women, on the other hand, regard manual and oral stimulation of their genitals equally favourably, but like intercourse best of all.

FANTASIES

A useful way of discovering the kinds of sexual activity that make people happy is to explore the contents of their sexual fantasies. The importance of these fantasies was attested to by a sex therapist who pointed out "Sex is composed of friction and fantasy." Sex fantasies are extremely common, forming the most frequent content of daydreams among young men and the second most frequent among middle-aged men. Even in the more sexually inhibited era of the 1940s, Alfred Kinsey and his colleagues reported that 84 per cent of males and 69 per cent of females had been aroused by fantasies involving the opposite sex. Nowadays the percentages of men and women having sexual fantasies is roughly equal, and rather higher than the figures reported by Kinsey. The increased prevalence of sexual fantasies may reflect the greater attention paid by the media to the topic of sex in all of its manifestations, but is more likely to be linked with the greater incidence of sexual activity in the population. The reason for favouring the latter explanation is that the sexually experienced are known to report many more sexual fantasies than virgins.

Which themes are most common in sexual fantasies? There are several themes favoured by a significant proportion of the population. Forty-five per cent of young British women fantasize about previous experiences during sexual activity, and 29 per cent fantasize about being raped or overpowered. Other themes include sex with more than one partner (21 per cent), sex with another woman (19 per cent), and various sexual activities with animals (10 per cent). The inventiveness of the human imagination means that there is a virtually infinite variety of activities that could form the basis of a sexual fantasy. However, it is easier to understand the main sources of sex fantasies if we assign them to a small number of broad categories. Exactly this approach was adopted by Glenn Wilson of the University of London. He identified four major categories of sex fantasy: exploratory; intimate; sadomasochistic; and impersonal (e.g. watching others having sex; being excited by leather or rubber). Since sadism and masochism are pretty much the opposite of each other, it might be thought that people having many sadistic fantasies would have relatively few masochistic fantasies, and vice versa. In fact, a study carried out in Germany among 245 male members of various sadomasochistic clubs found that most of the men concerned reported numerous fantasies of both a sadistic and a masochistic nature.

Which people have the most sex fantasies? The three characteristics most closely associated with numerous sex fantasies are experience with several different sex partners, high frequency of orgasm, and generally high sex drive. There are some interesting differences between men and women, most of which are in accord with stereotyped views. Whereas men are much more likely than women to report exploratory, sadomasochistic, and impersonal fantasies, women tend to favour sexual fantasies of an intimate nature.

The differences between the sex fantasies of men and women become even more striking when they are asked to single out the fantasy theme which they regard as the most exciting one of all. Women are most excited by intimate fantasies such as sex with a loved partner, kissing passionately, receiving oral sex, and making love out of doors in a romantic setting. In contrast, many men prefer fantasies of an exploratory nature, including promiscuous scenes, seduction, whipping and spanking, having sex with someone of a different race, or homosexuality. The way the evidence is shaping up it is beginning to look as if men and women differ more in their imaginary sexual exploits than in their actual sexual activities. The notion that the favourite sexual fantasies of men and women differ in major ways finds further support when men and women provide detailed descriptions of their favourite sexual fantasies. Those of men typically include information about anatomical details and possess a very strong visual emphasis. The women in their fantasies are usually anonymous figures, and the men do not feel emotionally involved with them. All of these findings merely serve to confirm the worst suspicions of women, who have always thought that men are immature in their dealings with the opposite sex. In contrast, women's favourite sexual fantasies typically involve some identifiable male figure such as the woman's husband or lover, or some famous man. For the most part, women experience considerable emotional involvement with the men in their fantasies. Unlike men's sexual fantasies, those of women rarely focus on the physical characteristics of their imagined sex partners.

Thus, the sexual fantasies of men and women could hardly be further apart. Men focus on physical appearance and tend to ignore what lies beneath the surface, whereas women do the exact opposite. In addition, men's fantasies reveal that they are sexually interested in numerous women who meet certain standards of physical attractiveness, whereas women are sexually interested in a specific man. This greater selectivity of women in their sexual fantasies helps to account for one of the largest differences between men and women in their sexual attitudes. When male and female students were asked whether they would take part in an orgy if asked to do so, 61 per cent of men said "Yes", against only 4 per cent of women. It is clear from these figures who is responsible for the dearth of orgies!

An issue that has stirred up a fair amount of disagreement and controversy is whether people who have many sexual fantasies are more or less happy and contented with their sex lives than those who have very few fantasies. Sigmund Freud was adamant that a lack of fantasies was the desirable state of affairs, because "A happy person never fantasizes, only an unsatisfied one." However, many people make use of sexual fantasies as a means of increasing their sexual excitement, and it could be argued quite reasonably that sexual fantasy adds to the richness and variety of one's sexual experiences.

There is some support for both points of view. Men who have a lot of sexual fantasies tend to be relatively dissatisfied with their sex lives, whereas women who fantasize extensively are generally rather satisfied with theirs.

Why is there this sex difference? Since we know that those who fantasize a lot about sex have relatively high sex drive, it is possible that men with numerous sexual fantasies resort to fantasies because they are unable to find enough available women to satisfy them. In contrast, women with high sex drive or libido and plentiful fantasies are unlikely to experience much difficulty in finding men quite prepared to satisfy their physical appetites. Alternatively, remember that women's fantasies often refer to concrete sexual activities that have actually happened or might happen in the future, and so are unlikely to provoke much dissatisfaction. Men's sexual fantasies, on the other hand, often revolve around unattainable perfections of feminine pulchritude, and these are likely to make mundane reality seem unappealing.

APHRODISIACS

An aspect of sexual activity which has received considerable media attention in recent years is the use of artificial means of enhancing sexual pleasure. For thousands of years people have been interested in the possibility that certain substances might act as aphrodisiacs, that is to say, they might increase sexual drive. The range of substances claimed to possess this magical power is almost limitless. There have been those who have been impressed by the splendidly erect horn of the rhinoceros, and have ground it up (the horn not the rhinoceros) in order to increase male potency. In Europe, a popular aphrodisiac over the centuries has been "Spanish fly", which is a substance made from a bright green beetle. Spanish fly may have romantic connotations, but it is in reality an extreme irritant to the mucous membranes of the urogenital tract. Even worse, it is poisonous if taken in large doses.

To cut a long story short, there is an almost total lack of evidence that any of the so-called aphrodisiacs actually affect sexuality or libido in the ways claimed for them. However, even if it must be concluded that aphrodisiacs as such do not exist, there is still a possibility that certain drugs or substances have the power to enhance sexual pleasure. The drugs that have been alleged to make sexual activities more pleasurable include the hallucinogens (such as LSD), marijuana or hash, and a number of central nervous system stimulants like cocaine or the amphetamines. Recently, great claims have been made for a drug called MDA (3, 4-methylenedioxyamphetamine), which has a chemical structure that is intermediate between that of the stimulant amphetamine and that of the hallucinogen mescaline. It has been argued on its behalf that MDA represents the best of both worlds, in that it combines the sexual enhancement of stimulant drugs with the empathy and self-insight of hallucinogens, but without the disturbances of thought found with other hallucinogens such as LSD. What is one to make of these claims? Since most of the drugs concerned are both illegal and potentially dangerous, there have been very few systematic attempts by psychologists to carry out the research that would be needed to answer that question. Despite the virtual absence of any relevant evidence, the American Medical Association's Committee on Human Sexuality reported in the 1970s that the enhanced pleasure produced by these drugs was merely a placebo effect. In other words, these drugs work because we think they are going to work, and not because of any intrinsic characteristics of the drugs themselves.

However, there are grounds for supposing that some of the reported effects are genuine. Physiological arousal is an important ingredient in sexual enjoyment, and it has been found that the most liked sexual activities are the ones that are most arousing. It follows that substances like cocaine and amphetamine which are central nervous system stimulants might well enhance sexual pleasure via heightened arousal. At an anecdotal level, many women who have never experienced an orgasm during sexual intercourse have done so after taking cocaine or amphetamine.

Rather more is known about marijuana or hash, which is taken by a very large number of people. When *Redbook Magazine* published a survey of 100,000 women, approximately one-third of them reported that they occasionally or frequently engaged in sexual activity shortly after smoking marijuana, with the figure being as high as 63 per cent among the women under the age of 20.

What exactly are the psychological effects of marijuana? There are consistent reports that it enhances the sensations experienced by the various sensory modalities, and this is especially true of touch and taste. However, the best-known effects of marijuana are that it loosens inhibitions, slows the perception of time, and greatly enhances sexual pleasure. Among middle-class, habitual users of hash, 58 per cent of the men and 32 per cent of the women claimed that it improved the quality and enjoyment of orgasm. Sexual desire increased in 60 per cent of women and 40 per cent of men after taking hash.

The apparent enhancement of sexual pleasure provided by marijuana seems rather paradoxical if one considers its effects at a physiological level. A major ingredient in marijuana is delta-9-tetrahydrocannabinol (THC), which suppresses production of the male sex hormone testosterone and can cause temporary impotence. In similar fashion, marijuana can disrupt the female menstrual cycle and even produce temporary sterility.

A drug that is used so extensively in the Western world that we often forget that it is a drug at all is ethyl alcohol or the demon drink. It has a mixed reputation in the sexual field. Men who drink a lot complain of "brewer's droop", but still ply their girl-friends with drink because of their belief that the conscience or superego is "dissoluble in alcohol". Of course, if alcohol is taken to excess, the effects on all of life's activities become detrimental. This has been known for a very long time. The Code of Hamurabi over 3500 years ago warned against alcohol abuse, and there are injunctions against excessive use of alcohol on the wall of the amphitheatre at Delphi in Greece. In small doses, however, alcohol often reduces feelings of stress and anxiety, and generally enhances mood.

Common sense tells us that small amounts of alcohol may facilitate sexual pleasure, but that large amounts are likely to be counterproductive. As so often happens, it transpires that common sense provides us with an over-simplified and inaccurate view of the world. Some of the complexities were revealed in a study in which young women were given fruit juice mixed with a little or a lot of vodka. After they had finished their drink, they watched a sexually explicit film, and then masturbated to orgasm. The women who had consumed the equivalent of three to five mixed drinks showed decreased orgasmic responding as indicated by various physiological measures. This is only to be expected, because alcohol acts as a central nervous system depressant. However, it is intriguing to note that relatively high alcohol intoxication produced reports of much greater sexual arousal and orgasmic pleasure, which is the opposite of the message provided by the physiological data. The complexities of these results are not matched by those with men, for whom drinking alcohol reduces both orgasmic intensity and sexual pleasure.

The latest word on the effects of alcohol is that they are surprisingly often not really due to the alcohol at all, but rather are placebo effects. In other words, alcohol has its effects simply because people expect it to have those effects. This has been shown by fooling people into believing that they are drinking alcohol. Under these circumstances, people become more relaxed, and women become more sexually responsive, even though they may have drunk only tonic water! This opens up interesting possibilities of obtaining the benefits of alcohol at negligible cost and with no subsequent hangover.

In sum, there is some evidence that many drugs can boost sexual pleasure, but the dangers of addiction and the illegality of nearly all of them should deter most people from trying them. The author's own advice (which unfortunately he is too lazy to follow himself) is to use a much simpler and safer approach based on physical exercise. Joggers and active players of sport have sex more frequently than their more sedentary fellows, and also enjoy it more.

PERSONALITY AND SEXUAL PLEASURE

So far we have not considered individual differences. We all know from personal experience that some people are much more interested in sex than others, and also derive more pleasure and happiness from it. Consider two celebrated examples. At one extreme, Mademoiselle Dubois who lived in the 18th century recorded a total of 16,527 lovers in 20 years, whereas Immanuel Kant never opened his account. We can make an educated guess about the kinds of people most and least likely to be interested in sexual behaviour on the basis of the discussion of personality in the last chapter. The pursuit of a member of the opposite sex often involves what is known as approach-avoidance conflict. There are potential rewards in the form of sexual favours and affection (that is the approach side), but there are also some potential negative consequences (e.g., being rejected or laughed at) which produce avoidance. The kind of person who will thrill to the chase is one who focusses on, or emphasizes, the potential rewards and at the same time minimizes the potential punishments. Extraverts tend to be optimistic and focus on rewards or positive affect, and those low in neuroticism or anxiety (i.e., stable people) are relatively unaffected by punishment or negative affect. It thus seems plausible that stable extraverts should be most interested in sexual activities, whereas neurotic introverts should be least interested.

My father, Hans Eysenck, carried out a major study in the 1970s into sexual attitudes. He discovered that there are two main dimensions to sexual attitudes: they are libido or sexual drive and satisfaction. Men scored somewhat higher than women on the sexual drive dimension, which fits in with the cultural stereotype. It also fits in with the results of a study of 210 marriages, in which approximately 35 per cent of the couples reported that the husband wanted sex more often than his wife, against only 7 per cent of the couples who reported the opposite.

In addition to the sex difference, there was also a tendency for extraverts to have higher sex drive than introverts, and for neurotic individuals to be more highly sexed than stable ones. However, there was a rather stronger relationship between libido and the personality dimension of psychoticism, which is a mixture of hostility and aggression.

Do these individual differences in sex drive affect actual sexual behaviour? There is strong evidence that they do. A large-scale study on over 6000 students carried out in West Germany reported especially powerful relationships between extraversion and sexual activity. For example, among the 19-year-old males, 45 per cent of extraverts had experienced sexual intercourse, against only 15 per cent of introverts. For female students of the same age, 29 per cent of extraverts had had sex, but only 12 per cent of introverts. Promiscuity was also much more prevalent among the extraverted students. Among those who were sexually active, 25 per cent of the extraverted males and 17 per cent of the extraverted females had had four or more sex partners during the preceding year, against 7 per cent of the introverted males and 4 per cent of the introverted females.

Extraverts do not differ from introverts only in the number of sexual partners. They also experiment with more positions for intercourse, they are more likely to pet to orgasm, and they engage in longer pre-coital foreplay. Among females, many more extraverts than introverts report that they nearly always experience orgasm during intercourse. The second major dimension of sexual attitudes is satisfaction, which is of course closely related to happiness. Anyone who is very satisfied with his or her sex life would indicate that their partner satisfies all of their physical needs, and that it is easy to tell their partner what they like or dislike about love-making, but they would deny that they worry about sex, that their love life is disappointing, that they have been deprived sexually, that they feel nervous with the opposite sex, that sexual feelings are unpleasant, and that sex jokes disgust them. A questionnaire of sexual attitudes including the above items was given to 423 male and 379 female university students aged between 18 and 22.

What would one expect to find? The satisfaction or happiness that different individuals derive from their sexual activities can easily be predicted on the basis of the discussion of personality in the last chapter. In essence, the argument put forward there was that stable or non-neurotic extraverts are happy people, whereas neurotic introverts are unhappy people. Since these characteristic individual differences in happiness seem to occur irrespective of the situation or circumstances, they should also be found in the sexual arena.

The findings were very much as predicted. Neurotic men and women were much less satisfied with their sex lives than were stable men and women (the correlation between neuroticism and satisfaction was nearly -0.5), and extraverted men and women were a lot more satisfied than introverted ones (the correlation between extraversion and satisfaction was approximately $+0.4$). In other words, men and women who are both stable and extraverted are very likely to feel happy and content about their sex lives, whereas neurotic introverts are as unhappy about their sex lives as they are about other things.

There are some very important implications of these findings. Many people have argued that sexual happiness can be indexed by the number of orgasms experienced or the amount of sex, or more plausibly on the extent to which one is lucky enough to find compatible boy-friends or girl-friends. These factors may all play some part in determining the happiness experienced through sexual activity, but the fact of the matter is that sexual happiness is firmly rooted in personality. In a nutshell, it is much more true to say that happy people make happy sex, rather than to claim that good sex makes people happy.

CHAPTER FOUR

Love and Marriage

WHAT IS LOVE?

In the words of the old saying, love makes the world go round. Whether that is true or not, it is undeniable that millions of people are willing to devote a huge amount of time and effort to the search for that elusive emotional state. The important role that love plays in our lives is suggested by the overwhelming emphasis on love in the lyrics of popular songs and in the romantic themes of best-selling books. The bulging newspaper columns of lonely hearts and the queues of people begging to have computers work out suitable partners for them attest to the feelings of deprivation experienced by those living without love in their lives. Some people have regarded love as being so crucial to them that they have been prepared to cheat, steal, and even murder in its name. Even if most people are not willing to go to those lengths, nearly everyone would agree that love is one of the best routes to achieving lasting happiness. As such, it merits detailed consideration in this book.

There may be general agreement that love is one of the major goals in life, but it is by no means clear that it means the same to everyone. For Shakespeare, love was "a spirit all compact of fire", whereas the journalist H. L. Mencken saw it as "a state of perceptual anaesthesia." One of the best-known definitions of love (but also one of the daftest and least convincing) was offered by the writer Erich Segal, who claimed that it is "not ever having to say you're sorry." Others have eschewed the conventional wisdom that love is a highly satisfactory state of affairs, and focussed on its dark side. Love has been thought of as a disease, or even a neurosis. The prominent Victorian poet Alfred Lord Tennyson was clearly thinking along these lines when he wrote of "the cruel madness of love."

What ought we to conclude about the nature of love in view of this diversity of opinion? The most obvious answer is to argue that there is some truth in all of these views, and that we must simply accept that love is a multi-dimensional state. Certainly we use the term "love" in many different ways in our everyday speech. We love the person we are married to or going out with, we love our country, and we also love our local football team and apple pie. Confronted with all of this vagueness of usage, one is tempted to agree with a gentleman rejoicing in the name of Finck. According to him, "Love is such a tissue of paradoxes, and exists in such an endless variety of forms and shades, that you may say almost anything about it that you please, and it is likely to be correct."

Despite all of the problems, several psychologists have refused to abandon the search for the central meaning of love. The Canadian sociologist J. A. Lee claimed that different couples have different styles of loving. There are three primary love styles, which he termed Eros, Storge, and Ludus. The Erotic style of love is based on immediate physical attraction, a fascination with beauty, sensuality, and good rapport between the two individuals involved. In contrast, Storge is a rather unexciting and undramatic love style. It involves affection and companionship, but is relatively devoid of passion. The third primary love style, Ludus, derives its name from the Latin word for "play". As that implies, Ludic lovers are hedonistic and unwilling to enter into long-term commitments.

J. A. Lee did not stop at the three primary love styles just described. He went on to identify three additional love styles that represent blends of the primary love styles. Eros and Storge in combination produce Agape, which is a dutiful and altruistic form of love in which the lover expects little in return. Storge and Ludus together make Pragma, which is a love style for the realistic and practical lover who actively seeks for a compatible partner. Finally, and most excitingly, there is Mania, which combines elements of Ludus and Eros. This love style is characterized by great emotional intensity in the form of obsession and jealousy.

J. A. Lee is on strong ground when he claims that loving couples evolve very different styles of interaction and emotional involvement. Some couples are overtly affectionate and "lovey-dovey" and spend all of their free time together, whereas other couples appear more formal and distant. What kinds of people find happiness in which styles of loving? As might be expected, men and women differ in their love styles. Men tend to be higher than women on Eros and Ludus, which is in line with the stereotypical view of men as higher than women in sex drive and their alleged unwillingness to become seriously committed to relationships. Women are on average more Pragmatic and Storgic than men, but they are also more Manic.

The notion that women are cooler and more calculating than men in affairs of the heart is the opposite of what is often believed. However, anyone who feels that women tend to be swept off their feet by the overpowering force of love may find the results of the following study sobering. Young adults were asked the question "If a boy (girl) had all the other qualities you desire, would you marry this person if you were not in love with him (her)?" Only about 35 per cent of young men would proceed with marriage on that basis, against approximately 70 per cent of young women.

The approach to love taken by J. A. Lee has a commonsensical feel about it, but it suffers from a number of limitations. One is that in these selfish times it is remarkably difficult to find anyone who adopts the altruistic or Agape style of love. More importantly, while Lee argued that he had discovered a number of very different love styles, it looks as if some of the styles differ from each other mainly in the amount rather than the kind of love experienced. Thus, Storge, Ludus, and Pragma all represent much more modest levels of love than Mania.

An alternative, and probably superior, way of conceptualizing love was put forward very recently by two American psychologists, Robert Sternberg and Susan Grajek. They argued controversially that the love that exists between two lovers, between parent and child, between siblings, and between best friends is fundamentally the same. Of course, they accepted that these love relationships differ in various obvious ways, such as the presence or absence of sexual desire, the involvement of feelings of responsibility, and the kinds of interaction which are feasible, but they claimed that these differences relate to the concomitants of love rather than to love itself.

Given this view of love, Robert Sternberg and Susan Grajek embarked on a search for the central core of love. What emerged as the crucial defining characteristics of love are interpersonal communication, sharing, and support. More specifically, love involves a deep understanding of the other person, sharing of information, ideas, and personal feelings, emotional support, personal growth, helping the partner, needing the other person and making him or her feel needed, and receiving and giving affection. The most striking finding was that all of these aspects of love are very important irrespective of the nature of the love relationship. Thus, the willingness to share with the other person and to provide emotional support are found in parents who love their children, in siblings who love each other, and in lovers involved in sexual relationships.

Armed with this analysis of the nature of love, Robert Sternberg and Susan Grajek set out to measure the amount of love that people feel for the different individuals whom they love. On average, one's partner in a heterosexual love relationship is the most loved person of all, followed by one's best friend, and then the members of one's immediate family (i.e., father, mother, and siblings), all of whom tend to be loved about equally.

There is a popular belief that each person has only a certain amount of love available to give, so that giving a lot to one person means that everyone else must receive less. In fact, those individuals who experience a great deal of love in one relationship actually tend to experience above average (rather than below average) love in all of their other love relationships, and this is especially true within families. Thus, some people are naturally much warmer and more loving than others, and they have ample love to give to everyone who matters deeply to them.

LOVE AND HAPPINESS

We are now in a position to consider the role played by love in promoting happiness within human relationships. In doing so, we will be relying heavily on the research that has been carried out in this area. While it seems clear to me that the only way we are ever likely to understand the mysterious workings of love is by means of systematic research, many prominent individuals have been actively hostile to the entire enterprise. Senator William Proxmire of Wisconsin was the chairman of the Senate committee keeping an eye on the activities of the National Science Foundation. When he found out that the Foundation had awarded a sizeable sum of money for research into the psychology of love, he reacted angrily: "Two hundred million Americans want to leave some things a mystery, and right at the top of those things we don't want to know is why a man falls in love with a woman and vice versa . . . I think it is time the National Science Foundation . . . rearranged its research priorities to address our scientific, not our erotic curiosity."

This is nonsense, and dangerous nonsense at that. In the first place, it is absurd to claim that people are not interested in understanding love. There have been literally thousands of articles in women's magazines which deal with the causes of, and cures for, romantic love and this reflects the public's insatiable interest in love in all of its manifestations. In the second place, there are enormous potential benefits to be gained in terms of human happiness if the research succeeds. This argument was expressed forcefully by the New York Times journalist James Reston: "If the sociologists and psychologists can get even a suggestion of the answer to our patterns of romantic love, marriage, disillusion, divorce—and the children left behind—it could be the best investment of Federal money since Mr. Jefferson made the Louisiana Purchase."

Men and women, boys and girls, who form long-term romantic relationships with each other typically report that these relationships are started and maintained because of the love which the two partners feel for each other. This can hardly be the whole story, because most romantic relationships are also based on friendship and liking. Does the success of a relationship and the happiness it produces depend more on love or on liking? One could argue that it is love that gives a romantic relationship its special quality, and therefore love is the key ingredient. On the other hand, if two people are to spend a long time together in a happy and agreeable manner, then it would seem almost essential that they like each other. Indeed, the combination of love with little liking produces an explosive mixture leading to frequent rows and unhappiness.

Before we can decide whether love or liking is the crucial ingredient in successful romantic relationships, we need to have some way of distinguishing between them. Zick Rubin has produced separate love and liking scales. His love scale is based on the assumption that love involves attachment (e.g., "If I could never be with ---, I would feel miserable"), caring (e.g.,"If --- were feeling badly, my first duty would be to cheer him (her) up"), and intimacy (e.g., "I feel very possessive toward ---"). The liking scale, on the other hand, has items concerning whether the other person is likeable, responsible, has the ability to earn respect, makes a favourable initial impression, and is the sort of person you would like to be.

It could be argued against Rubin that loving and liking are not really separate from each other, but rather that loving just represents an unusually high level of liking. This argument was refuted by Marshall Diener and Thomas Pyszczynski. They claimed that love differs from liking in that sexual feelings are much more closely related to love, and they chased up the implications of this claim in an ingenious study. Young men who were currently in love were asked to read either a boring description of the mating and courtship behaviour of herring gulls or a "Collegiate Fantasy". The Collegiate Fantasy story dealt in a very explicit way with the sexual fantasies and behaviour of a female student, including mutual fondling with a man, cunnilingus, and fellatio. Immediately after they had read one of these stories, the young men indicated their love and liking for their girl-friend on Rubin's scales. The sexually arousing story greatly increased feelings of love, but it had no effect at all on how much their girl-friend was liked. It seems reasonable that there is a weak link between liking and sexual feelings if you consider the things you think and say in a sexual context. Most people would not murmur "You have the ability to earn respect" during moments of great passion, but they might well say, "I love you."

Use of Rubin's love and liking scales has produced the counter-intuitive finding that the amount of liking is the single most important factor in determining the success and happiness of a relationship, with the amount of love being rather less important. This conflicts with the common belief that love is of central importance in romantic relationships (e.g., "Love conquers all"). However, day-day-day existence with another person is much more likely to be happy and contented if there is genuine liking and compatibility. Love without liking often leads to the plaintive cry, "I can't live without him (her), and I can't live with him (her)."

HOW CAN LOVE BE INCREASED?

Even if love is not the be-all and the end-all of a happy romantic relationship, it nevertheless makes a major contribution. The mysteries of love are still poorly understood, and it is by no means clear why we are attracted to some members of the opposite sex but not others. However, it may be possible to answer a somewhat simpler question that has occupied the minds of many people interested in increasing the sum of human happiness: how can love within a relationship be enhanced? The most influential answer was provided by Sigmund Freud, who argued as follows: "Some obstacle is necessary to swell the tide of libido (i. e., sexual energy) to its height, and at all periods of history whenever natural barriers in the way of satisfaction have not sufficed, mankind has erected conventional ones in order to enjoy love."

Very much the same notion was expressed in a much more poetic way by the Greek writer Vassilikos: "Once upon a time there was a little fish who was a bird from the waist up and who was madly in love with a little bird who was a fish from the waist up. So the Fish-Bird kept saying to the Bird-Fish: 'Oh, why were we created so that we can never live together? You in the wind and I in the wave. What a pity for both of us.' And the Bird-Fish would answer: 'No, what luck for both of us. This way we'll always be in love because we'll always be separated.'"

Most romantic books and films make use of the basic idea that difficulties and obstacles enhance love. The hero and heroine typically have to work their way through a whole series of problems which test their love before everything is finally sorted out and they live happily ever after. Perhaps the most famous fictional example of great lovers confronting enormous hindrances to their love is the relationship between

Romeo and Juliet. The way in which their love triumphed over the total opposition they experienced from their two feuding families inspired psychologists to investigate the "Romeo and Juliet effect". Young couples who either experienced or did not experience parental interference were compared. There were many different reasons for parental interference, ranging from a racial difference to the young man's shaggy appearance, and from the couple living together to a parental belief that their daughter could do better for herself. Regardless of the reason for the interference, those couples exposed to it were more deeply in love than couples free from parental interference.

Why does love grow in response to obstacles? The phenomenon may resemble that of private patients who react to the excessive fees charged by their doctor by arguing, "He must be an outstanding doctor!" Thus, lovers who are experiencing many hassles from their parents may think to themselves: "I really must be in love to put up with all of these hassles."

The discussion of emotion in Chapter Two suggests a rather different way in which sexual attraction and love can be increased. In general terms, the intensity of an emotional experience depends on the amount of physiological arousal associated with it. Since the nature of this physiological arousal does not vary much from one emotion to another, it follows that love can be enhanced by arousal stemming from an irrelevant source. This may explain the recommendation of Roman experts on love during classical times that young men should take ladies they were interested in to gladiatorial contests. The notion was that the ladies would misattribute the general excitement and arousal generated by events in the arena to the sexual attractiveness of their male companions.

This line of argument may seem rather simple-minded and fanciful. However, Joanne Cantor obtained evidence in its favour, and also discovered a complication. She showed young men excerpts from a "blue" film called *Naked Under Leather*. Those who had finished vigorous bicycle pedalling five minutes before viewing the film found it more sexually arousing than those who had just stopped pedalling. While both groups were highly aroused during the film, the latter group attributed their arousal to the after-effects of the exercise, and so did not feel sexually aroused by the film. In contrast, the former group did not link their aroused state during the film to the exercise they had had, and so misattributed their arousal to the film. Thus, sexual arousal requires physiological arousal, but it also depends on the precise interpretation of that arousal.

WHO FALLS IN LOVE?

In our discussion of the love experience, we have not as yet considered the issue of which kinds of people fall in love most and least often. Since love is basically a happy and positive emotion, we might expect that individuals who are generally happy (i.e., stable extraverts) would be most susceptible to love. There is some truth in this notion, because stable extraverts report more love experiences than other people. They also report the highest levels of love during the early stages of a romantic relationship.

In spite of these findings, there are many reasons why people fall in love, and it has been argued that unhappy people are most vulnerable to Cupid's arrows. According to the clinical psychologist Theodore Reik, dissatisfied people have unfulfilled needs which they hope that their romantic partner can satisfy. In their desperation, they incorporate their partner into their secret fantasies, and experience all of the pangs of love. As this analysis would suggest, unhappy people (i.e., neurotic introverts) experience the greatest intensity of love, and find it more mysterious and less controllable than other people do.

WAXING AND WANING OF LOVE

Whatever the reasons for people falling in love, it is probably unrealistic to hope that love can be maintained at peak level for very long. Why exactly this should be so is unclear. However, the cynical observation of George Bernard Shaw that love is "a gross exaggeration of the difference between one person and everybody else" may hold the key. Sooner or later we all discover that our loved one is not the "knight in shining armour" or the "fairy-tale princess" that we had initially supposed, and the intrusion of reality typically reduces love. It may be for this reason that it has been suggested that, "the history of a love affair is the drama of its fight against time."

Since most of us feel that we can judge the character of other people reasonably well, it does seem somewhat puzzling that we so often seem to over-value those with whom we become emotionally involved. Of course, part of the reason is probably that our intense emotional feelings prevent our normal critical faculties from functioning properly, but there are intriguing indications that there may be more to it than that. Perhaps what is of prime importance is a self-fulfilling prophecy: if I think that you may be wonderful and sexually alluring, then the positive and encouraging way I behave towards you may help you to confirm my initial impression. Thus, our romantic partners may actually behave in particularly agreeable and charming ways during the early stages of courtship, but our mistake is to under-estimate the significance of our own behaviour in eliciting the best from them.

This notion of a self-fulfilling prophecy was put to the test in a study in which young men talked on the phone with an unknown girl whom they believed to be either physically attractive or physically unattractive. In fact, it was the same girl in either case. The men's expectation or "prophecy" was that the attractive girl would be much more sociable, humorous, socially adept, and poised than the unattractive girl. Lo and behold, when the girl was talking with men who had been told she was physically attractive, she spoke in a way that was sociable, humorous, socially adept, and poised! Further analysis based on tape recordings revealed that the men used different conversational styles with the allegedly attractive and unattractive girls: they were considerably more sociable, sexually warm, and interesting when they thought they were speaking to the physically attractive girl.

There is a moral to be drawn from this study. Those who complain angrily or sadly that their romantic partner has changed may well be right in the sense that his or her behaviour within the relationship is no longer the same as it used to be. However, the change may depend far more on the altered behaviour of the person who is complaining than on anything else.

If, for whatever reason, intense love cannot be relied on to keep a romantic relationship in good shape, then we must look for other factors that can. One that has been claimed to be particularly important is the extent to which the relationship is a fair and equitable one. This may sound implausible for a number of reasons. The popular view is that, while a mundane consideration such as fairness matters a lot in friendships, it is of little relevance to love affairs. Lovers do not usually keep a careful check on how much they are giving to, and receiving from, the relationship. Moreover, the normal rules of friendship do not apply because there is a kind of "we-feeling", in which the pleasures and pains of one's partner are experienced as one's own.

Despite all of these arguments, the fact remains that fairness or equity in a relationship has a major effect on its success. Where there is inequity in a love relationship, one individual is "under-benefitted", whereas the other is "over-benefitted". For example, if a married women works full-time in order to permit her husband to gain professional qualifications, and he responds by asking for a divorce as soon as his examinations are over, then she is clearly substantially under-benefitted. Those who put much more into a relationship than they get out of it are likely to be very angry. What about the over-benefitted person in the relationship? He or she may be delighted in some ways to be so fortunate, but the knowledge that they do not deserve their good fortune tends to make them feel guilty and uncomfortable.

In contrast to the negative emotions produced by inequity, the knowledge that one is in a balanced and equitable relationship offers the potential of lasting happiness. It has been found that couples in equitable relationships are more likely to stay together, and to feel happy with the relationship. In inequitable relationships, the under-benefitted person is especially unhappy, but the over-benefitted person is also fairly unhappy. These effects are found even during the "honeymoon period" that follows marriage: newly-weds in inequitable marriages are angry, guilty, and discontented.

A final factor that is of great importance in determining the duration and happiness of a love affair is the general similarity betweend the two people involved. There are two popular but opposed views about the role that similarity plays. On the one hand, some believe that "Opposites attract", whereas others hold that "Birds of a feather flock together." The latter proverb is much closer to the mark, as was shown in a major American study of student romantic couples. Over the two-year period of the study, approximately half of the couples remained together. Those who stayed together were more similar in several ways than those who did not, including physical attractiveness, career plans, intelligence, and age. When the couples who had broken up were asked to say why the relationship had ended, differences in sexual attitudes, interests, backgrounds, and ideas were frequently mentioned.

JEALOUSY

We have seen that liking, love, equity, and similarity all contribute to the success and happiness of romantic relationships. Of the factors that are destructive of relationships, one of the most potent is jealousy. The potentially tragic consequences of jealousy were described by Shakespeare with great psychological insight in his play *Othello*. The devious Iago makes Othello suspicious that his wife Desdemona has been unfaithful to him with a young Florentine called Cassio, although these suspicions have no basis in fact. When Iago then arranges matters so that a precious handkerchief which Othello had given to Desdemona is discovered in the possession of Cassio, Othello's jealousy becomes extreme and he kills Desdemona in her bed. The power of irrational jealousy to produce extreme patterns of behaviour has been labelled the "Othello syndrome".

It may be argued that Othello's reactions to his feelings of jealousy are a sign of complete madness. However, it is noteworthy that a great majority of murders are committed by one member of a family on another member of the same family, and that many of these murders involve jealousy to a greater or a lesser extent. Police files on murders committed in Detroit during the early 1970s indicated that approximately one-sixth had jealousy as the motive.

While jealousy is rarely of the burning intensity that leads to murder, it appears to be surprisingly prevalent, at least among the young. Sixty-three per cent of young male students and 51 per cent of young female students in one study admitted that they were currently jealous. Whether or not all of this jealousy has a positive side to it is an issue that has attracted a lot of controversy. One popular view is that jealousy does serve to demonstrate the intense feelings of love experienced by the jealous person, since we would hardly become jealous of a rival who threatened to take away someone who meant little to us. An early advocate of this point of view was Andreas Capellanus, the 12th century author of *The Art of Courtly Love*. He argued that jealousy is "the very substance of love . . . lovers should always welcome it as the mother and the nurse of love."

Nowadays it is more fashionable to emphasize the notion that jealousy is a self-defeating emotion that serves to make both the jealous person and his or her lover unhappy. According to this line of reasoning, jealousy is a "green-eyed monster" that afflicts only the chronically unstable and neurotic individual. The case for the prosecution was put very forcefully by O'Neill and O'Neill: "The more insecure you are, the more you will be jealous. Jealousy, says Abraham Maslow, 'practically always breeds further rejection and deeper insecurity.' And jealousy, like a destructive cancer, breeds more jealousy. It is never, then, a function of love but of our insecurities and dependencies. It is the fear of a loss of love and it destroys that very love. It is detrimental to and a denial of a loved one's personal identity. Jealousy is a serious impediment, then, to the development of security and identity."

Common sense suggests that both points of view are partially correct. The notion that jealousy is a fairly natural consequence of love rather than merely a sign of insecurity receives some support from the very large numbers of people who experience it. If someone's dreams of future happiness with their lover seems likely to be dashed to the ground by a sexual rival, it would seem rather difficult not to become jealous. On the other hand, the woman who becomes jealous and certain that her husband is having an affair if he arrives home ten minutes later than usual is manifestly acting in a way which reflects her insecurities.

Both men and women who are deeply in love are much more likely to report jealous feelings than those who are less emotionally attached. However, the extent to which one likes one's current partner has no effect at all on the amount of jealousy experienced. Jealousy is also affected by insecurity, since women who score high on neuroticism are considerably more jealous than their relatively stable counterparts. Jealous women also tend to be introverted. In contrast, jealous men are a little more neurotic than non-jealous men, but the two groups do not differ in extraversion.

It is not clear why individual differences in personality should play a more prominent role in determining jealousy levels in women than in men. However, it is interesting that jealousy in women can be accounted for in a general way by the theoretical ideas discussed in Chapter Two. It was argued there that stable extraverts have the "happiness gene" and neurotic introverts have the "unhappiness gene". Since jealousy is a prime example of an emotional state producing great unhappiness and misery, it follows that neurotic introverts should be most susceptible to jealousy and stable extraverts least susceptible. That, of course, is precisely the pattern of individual differences in jealousy found in women.

The $64,000 question in the area of jealousy is which sex experiences more jealousy. From the macho perspective, it could be argued that the potential or actual loss of his girl-friend or wife constitutes more of an affront to a man's pride than does the loss of her boy-friend or husband to a woman. On the other hand, the greater emotionality and vulnerability of women may make them experience the pangs of jealousy more than men. In fact, men and women differ very little in susceptibility to jealousy, perhaps because the factors above cancel each other out. Where the two sexes do differ, however, is in the ways they behave when they are jealous. The typical jealous male reacts with anger and with threats to terminate the relationship, whereas the jealous female is more likely to react with depression and/or attempts to improve the quality of the relationship.

LIVING TOGETHER

In days gone by, the stages of heterosexual attachment could readily be identified. Romantic love followed the earlier stages of casual and serious dating, followed in turn by engagement and marriage. Nowadays, there are more options open to people in Western society, and the most obvious example of this is the startling increase in what is known technically as cohabitation. Cohabitation or living together is a mode of living that characterizes approximately eight million Americans at the present time, and it is even more popular among the Scandinavians.

There are many different reasons why people choose to defy convention and, as they say, "live in sin." Four patterns of cohabitation have been identified among university students. For some, living together satisfies the need for one of the partners to be involved in a relationship, whereas for others it provides the convenience of domestic living, or it is a symbol of emancipation. For the remainder, it represents a new stage in the courtship sequence that runs from dating throught to marriage.

In general, those who cohabit seem to be reasonably happy with their chosen life-style. Cohabiting and engaged couples show approximately the same degree of commitment to their relationships, whereas one might have expected those living together to be less committed to each other than those firmly intending to get married. When cohabiting couples were compared with married couples in terms of satisfaction and happiness, no real differences emerged. It is thus abundantly clear that cohabitation has become a viable alternative to marriage for many people.

In view of the fact that living together is still regarded in many quarters as a threat to the fabric of society, it comes as no surprise to discover that people who live together tend to be unconventional in other ways as well. Cohabitors are more likely than non-cohabitors to be interested in astrology, extra-sensory perception, and the occult. They are also more likely to be vegetarian, to use illicit drugs, and to go to rock festivals. This unconventionality extends into the sexual field. People who live together engage in a disproportionate amount of oral and group sex, and female cohabitors are more likely than female non-cohabitors to initiate sexual activities.

In sum, living together is an unconventional life-style which tends to appeal to unconventional people. While cohabitation would probably not suit most people, it provides a perfectly happy and sensible way of living for many people. This is perhaps especially true for people who have been divorced, and who as a result are wary of further marital involvement on the principle of "once bitten, twice shy."

LOVE AND MARRIAGE

The growing popularity of cohabitation and increased sexual licence does not mean, as has sometimes been claimed, that marriage is on the way out. In most Western countries, over 90 per cent of the population marry at least once in their lives. Even though more marriages than ever end in divorce, most divorced people re-marry within five years. Thus, the great majority of people spend most of their adult lives in the married state. Why do people dash like lemmings into marriage? George Bernard Shaw, the master of paradox, expressed some legitimate doubts about the value of marriage: "Those who talk about the blessings of marriage and the constancy of its vows are the very people who declare that if the chains were broken and the prisoners left free to choose, the whole social fabric would fly asunder. You cannot have the argument both ways. If the prisoner is happy, why lock him in? If he is not, why pretend that he is?"

The traditional Western view is that the main reason for a boy and a girl getting married is because they are deeply in love with each other. In the words of the old song, "Love and marriage, love and marriage, go together like a horse and carriage." This view of marriage is greeted with an indulgent chuckle by those who have studied marriage customs in other cultures. Our limited perspective on marriage was emphasized by the sociologist Ralph Linton: "All societies recognize that there are occasional violent emotional attachments between persons of the opposite sex, but our present American culture is practically the only one which has attempted to capitalize on these and make them the basis for marriage. The hero of the modern American movie is always a romantic lover, just as the hero of an old Arab epic is always an epileptic. A cynic may suggest that in an ordinary population the percentage of individuals with capacity for romantic love of the Hollywood type was about as large as that of persons able to throw genuine epileptic fits."

Ralph Linton wrote the above 50 years ago, and there are signs that the emphasis on love as the major basis for marriage is declining. When engaged couples were asked a few years ago what they hoped marriage would offer, they came up with a variety of specific answers. The most popular reason for getting married was the companionship it appeared to offer, with the prospect of having healthy and happy children being the second most common answer. Two other frequently given reasons were to have a satisfactory sex life, and to live in a home where one belonged.

While many people put forward perfectly sensible and logical reasons for taking the big step of entering into the matrimonial state, there are a surprisingly large number of people who stumble into marriage in a rather casual fashion. A good example of this is the case of a young working-class man in America, who described his erratic progress towards the altar in the following way: "We met at this place and I kind of liked her. She was cool and kind of fun to be with. Before I knew it we were going steady. I had this class ring from high school and she kept wanting me to give it to her. So finally one night I took it off and did . . . She made a big thing of it, and so did her family. Don't get me wrong; I liked her good enough. But I just didn't think about getting married—not then anyhow. But then, after we had been going together for almost a year, it just seemed like the thing to do. So we did."

Notice that the word "love" is conspicuously absent from the above account. Many experts argue that, as in the above example, relatively mundane considerations loom large in the marriage stakes. This view was expressed in somewhat cynical terms by the famous sociologist, Erving Goffman. He claimed that a proposal of marriage "tends to be the way in which a man sums up his social attributes and suggests to a woman that hers are not so much better as to preclude a merger or partnership in these matters." It is perhaps unappealing to conclude that the rules of the market-place apply to young men and women seeking a marriage partner, but such a conclusion is certainly consistent with much of the evidence. The overall attractiveness of a husband and his wife tends to be quite similar. They generally belong to the same social class and race, and are approximately equal in terms of physical attractiveness and intelligence. Of particular interest are married couples where the husband differ substantially in, say, physical attractiveness. Exactly as the market-place metaphor would suggest, the less attractive member of the married couple typically "makes up" for his or her physical deficiencies by being rich or particularly self-sacrificing. An example of this kind of trade-off is the marriage between Carlo Ponti and Sophia Loren, where he contributes wealth and talent and she contributes great beauty.

Other forms of trade-off are also fairly common. Working-class girls who marry "above themselves" are on average considerably more physically attractive than those who do not. What is happening here is that the husband brings his superior social standing to the marriage, while his wife enhances the marriage with her beauty.

Whether people marry for love, for social standing, for companionship, or for some other reason, they presumably all anticipate that the married state will be happier and more enjoyable than the single state. That millions of people should think along these lines is at first sight rather strange. The mixed blessings of marriage have been extensively documented in the media over recent years, and have revealed a previously unsuspected depth of misery associated with many people's marriages. Approximately half of the families in England have experienced at least one incident of physical violence between husband and wife, and 28 per cent of families report one or more violent acts during the preceding year. Statistics like these led the psychologist Robert Burgess to focus on the depressing side of the marriage state: "Conflicts of interest are infinite in number and are the grist for escalating disengagement, disaffection, and domestic guerilla warfare."

Of course, marriage does have some things to recommend it. It can provide love, companionship, and a sound foundation for family life. Given the obvious advantages and disadvantages of the married state, it is not easy to decide whether married people are generally happier than those who remain single. However, there is a popular stereotype that married women are happier than single women, with the latter turning into unattractive and frustrated spinsters, but single men are happier than married men because they are free and sexually promiscuous.

The evidence assembled by psychologists refutes most of these popular views. The value of marriage as an institution has been called into question by feminists, sociologists, and the like, and yet married people are considerably happier on average than those who are not married. Thirty-five per cent of married men and 38 per cent of married women say they are "very happy", which compares most favourably with never-married men and women (18 per cent in both cases). Of those who have ever been married but are now separated, divorced, or widowed, an even smaller percentage is "very happy", falling as low as 7 per cent for separated and widowed men. In other words, married men are five times as likely as separated or widowed men to be very happy, and they are three times as likely as divorced men to be very happy. The same pattern, although with less striking differences, is true for women.

It thus looks as if marriage is actually good for you! This conclusion is strengthened by having a look at the percentages of people who admit that they are "not too happy". Under 10 per cent of married people are "not too happy", but a massive 40 per cent of separated people are "not too happy", as well as over 30 per cent of divorced people.

Those who have never been married are less happy than married people, but happier than those who have been married but are no longer in that state, with approximately 17 per cent being "not too happy". In other words, marriage seems to prevent people from becoming unhappy as well as actively promoting their happiness.

In what ways are the unmarried less happy with their lot than the married? Perhaps marriage provides an emotional and social setting that increases positive affect, or perhaps marriage reduces negative affect by enabling problems to be shared, providing sympathy and understanding, and preventing loneliness. In fact, married people generally report more positive affect and less negative affect than the unmarried. Among the unmarried, there are some interesting effects involving positive and negative affect. Single men and women are comparably happy, but single men have greater negative affect than single women, whereas single women have less positive affect than single men. In other words, single men tend to experience more emotional highs and lows than single women.

Of course, it would make little sense to argue that marriage provides a magic cure for unhappiness. Indeed, as everyone would expect, the evidence is very clear that a poor marriage is actually less conducive to happiness than no marriage at all. Only four per cent of those who are not too happily married report that their lives are "very happy", which is a smaller percentage than for any of the unmarried groups.

It is sometimes argued that marriage is more central in the lives of women than of men. While the pattern is gradually changing, it is still true that married men tend to spend more of their time away from the family home than married women because of their work and leisure-time activities. As would be expected, the association between marital happiness and overall happiness is rather greater for married women than for their husbands. Indeed, many married women more or less seem to equate their happiness in life with the quality of the marital relationship.

Marriage is not only of more importance to wives than to husbands, but it also seems to be more stressful for them. Part of the reason may be because women have to make more adjustments than men when they get married, with the advent of children often producing dramatic changes in their daily routine. The substantial adaptation that women have to make in marriage has sometimes been described as a "Pygmalion effect", and it may be this that makes married women have more neurotic symptoms and lower self-esteem than single women. In contrast, men seem to thrive on marriage. Married men live longer, have superior mental health, lower suicide rates, and better career prospects than their single counterparts. Not surprisingly, married men tend to be happier than married women with their marriages, and wives are more likely than husbands to contemplate divorce and to initiate divorce proceedings.

When we think in more detail about the determinants of marital happiness, it is useful to remember that happiness consists of a combination of high positive affect and low negative affect. Sexual intercourse is one of the major sources of positive affect in a marriage, and rows and arguments can produce much negative affect. This suggests that a crude predictor of marital happiness could be constructed by simply subtracting the rate of arguments from the rate of intercourse. This measure turns out to be surprisingly useful. Married couples who usually have more rows than acts of intercourse often separate or divorce because of the unhappy state of their marriage, whereas most couples who have intercourse much more often than they have arguments are fairly or very happy in their marriages.

Of course, the happiness that marriage provides tends to fluctuate over time. Sadly, the most usual pattern is for happiness to decline progressively throughout the early years of marriage. It was found in one study that approximaterly three-quarters of newly-wed men and women described their spouses in positive and glowing terms, but many women soon become disenchanted. Only 42 per cent of middle-aged wives express a positive opinion of their husbands, and 16 per cent describe their husbands in a negative and disapproving way. Interestingly, the husbands do not share their wives' disillusionment (or do not dare to tell the truth). Eighty-five per cent of middle-aged husbands describe their wives in favourable terms, and practically none of them is seriously critical. A hopeful sign for any middle-aged man currently suffering from a disapproving wife is that married women of 60 and above tend to become more contented with their lot. As many as 82 per cent of women in this age group are reasonably positive in their assessment of their husbands.

A major change that the great majority of married couples experience comes about with the patter of little feet. What effects do children have on the happiness levels of their parents? Some people have argued that children make a marriage, whereas those of a more cynical disposition claim that children are more likely to break a marriage. At least in the United States of America, children tend to reduce a married couple's happiness. This is true for both men and women, but especially women. It is also true for all religious groups, races, and educational levels. The only group of people whose happiness does not suffer from having children consists of white people who feel that the ideal number of children in a family is at least four, but even here there is no indication that children actually enhance parental happiness! On top of all of these findings, it also appears that married couples become happier again when their children have left the family nest. Older women whose children are still living at home are more self-pitying, easily hurt, dissatisfied, and touchy than women of the same age whose children have all left home.

What on earth is going on here? Can it really be the case that the human race continues only because there is widespread ignorance of the adverse effects of children on happiness? There are at least two reasons for not accepting that implausible conclusion. Firstly, the presence of children undoubtedly deters many unhappily married people from divorcing, whereas married couples without children are likely to separate or divorce if they are unhappy with each other. Those couples who decide to stay together "for the sake of the children" may be creating the impression that children are bad for you. Secondly, what makes life satisfying and of value is not simply the amount of happiness experienced. Speaking as someone with three children of my own, I would argue strongly that children make life richer and more worthwhile, even if they do not boost the overall level of happiness.

CHAPTER FIVE

Happiness in Society

In this chapter, we take a somewhat broader view than before, and examine the levels of happiness or well-being within society. We also consider some of the factors which may contribute to, or detract from, the well-being of members of a society. A point of view which has exercised a powerful influence on the thinking of politicians over the past 100 years or so, and continues to do so even today, is that people can be made happier by giving them extra spending power. However, this ignores the very real costs which are incurred in forming a consumer society. The pollution and scarred landscapes produced as by-products of expanding production may mean that the overall quality of life is actually reduced even though people have more money in their pockets.

This emphasis on the quality of life clearly represents an advance over an exclusive focus on material possessions, but it still seems inadequate. The only effective way of assessing people's quality of life is to ask them. Often this is not done, because politicians and other influential people are unduly confident that they understand the factors which increase and decrease the quality of life. They may feel that reducing pollution and improving the standard of living will make people happy with the quality of their lives, but it is clearly advisable to check this out with them. As Marcus Aurelius pointed out many centuries ago, "No man is happy who does not think himself so."

DEMOGRAPHIC FACTORS

When politicians and others making decisions about social policy consider the impact of their policies, they usually divide up the population along demographic lines, taking account of such obvious characteristics as age, sex, race, and so on. This demographic approach has also appealed to a number of psychologists interested in investigating happiness or well-being within society. During the late 1960s and 1970s, several large-scale studies looked at large random samples of the American population with respect to the factors associated with well-being or its lack. Across these studies, the opinions of over 10,000 people were obtained, so that we now have a firm understanding of some of the general reasons why some groups of people are happy whereas others are unhappy.

As you might imagine, there are great differences from one person to the next in terms of how contented they are with their lives. Frank Andrews and Stephen Withey asked 1297 American adults the following question: "How do you feel about life in the United States today?" Seven per cent said they were "delighted", and a further 22 per cent were "pleased", but 5 per cent were "mostly dissatisfied" and 4 per cent felt "unhappy" or "terrible" In general, more people seem to be happy than unhappy. In other studies, approximately one-third of those asked whether they are "very happy", "pretty happy", or "not too happy" indicated that they were "very happy", against only 10 per cent who were "not too happy."

When we look at possible demographic reasons for the fact that some people are happier than others, all of the researchers have reached the same somewhat surprising conclusion: none of the major demographic factors such as age, sex, income socio-economic status, and race is at all strongly related to the level of happiness. Thus, the prevalent view that young people of high socio-economic status earning good money are likely to be much happier than older people of low socio-economic status living in poverty is much less true than one might have supposed. The relative ineffectiveness of demographic variables in influencing happiness was shown particularly clearly by Angus Campbell, Philip Converse, and Willard Rodgers. They looked at the effects of ten different factors on happiness levels in 2164 men and women. The factors they considered were age, race, in work or not, family income, occupation of the head of the household, education, religion, sex, urbanicity, and stage of the life cycle (e.g., unmarried; married without children; married with children). Using all ten factors together only allowed Campbell and his associates to account for 10 per cent of the variation in happiness between one person and another. Not surprisingly, they concluded that "the major determiners of well-being are psychological rather than economic or demographic."

These findings fit in well with the arguments put forward in Chapter Two. It was suggested there that happiness depends mainly on the kind of personality or character you inherit, which of course implies that the precise circumstances in which you live are of relatively little consequence. However, we should not totally ignore the demographic factors. If one examines matters closely, it turns out that some factors are definitely more important than others in affecting well-being and happiness. Among these more important factors are age, family life-cycle stage, socio-economic status, family income, and occupational status, whereas sex, race, religion, and education are all largely irrelevant to happiness.

Age

Common sense suggests that younger people are generally happier than older people, and there is an element of truth in this commonsensical view. Norman Bradburn discovered that 38 per cent of people in their twenties described themselves as "very happy", against 31 per cent of those in their thirties, and 30 per cent of those in their forties and fifties. In terms of those who were "not too happy", only 8 per cent of those in their twenties fell into this category, with the figures increasing progressively decade by decade up to 17 per cent of those in their fifties.

One of the most insightful analyses of the effects of age on happiness was reported by Marjorie Lowenthal, Majda Thurher, David Chiriboga and their associates. They focussed their attention on people in transition at four different stages of life: students in their last two years at school; young newly-weds; middle-aged parents with an average age of 50; and people preparing for retirement with an average age of 60. When these groups were all asked which point in life they considered to be the best, approximately 60 per cent chose adolescence or their twenties. However, most of the enthusiasm for early adulthood was shown by those who were themselves young, and only one-third of the middle-aged and pre-retirement groups chose that period of life. A more revealing way of describing the findings is to note that half of the people selected a time within five years of their present age. The kind of thinking that produced this result is illustrated by the answer given by a middle-aged woman with children: "Best age? Oh dear, that's a hard question.   Oh, I would say in your forties, when your children are practically grown; then you don't have many responsibilities. You are set in life and you have enough to be comfortable."

Further interesting light was shed on how age affects people by asking each of the four groups to indicate which of 70 adjectives applied to themselves. The major finding was that people seem to feel that they become better as they get older. There were 18 adjectives which were selected less often with increasing age, and 16 of them were undesirable. The desirable adjectives were dramatic and shrewd, and the undesirable adjectives were as follows: absent-minded, dependent, disorderly, dissatisfied, easily embarrassed, guileful, helpless, lazy, restless, sarcastic, self-pitying, stubborn, suspicious, timid, undecided, and unhappy. In addition, three desirable attributes were selected more often with increasing age: frank, self-controlled, and reserved.

What is a little strange is the apparent discrepancy between these findings and ratings of well-being and happiness. On the one hand, people tend to feel more satisfied about themselves and their personalities as they grow older, but, on the other hand, they are generally less happy with their lives. Part of the reason why older people are less happy may be the reduced time they have available for being with their friends. In the first place, the number of friends one has tends to decrease throughout much of life. Newlyweds have an average of 7.6 friends, but middle-aged parents have only 4.7 friends on average. Furthermore, while students at school usually interact daily with their friends, newly-weds and middle-aged people are more likely to see their friends on a weekly or a monthly basis.

In order to understand more clearly exactly the effects of age on happiness, it is important to remember that happiness can most appropriately be regarded as a combination of high positive affect and low negative affect. This means that the greater happiness of young people may be due to their greater capacity for positive affect, to their lower capacity to experience negative affect, or to a combination of the two. Marjorie Lowenthal and her associates assessed whether those in each of their four different age groups were high or low on positive and negative experiences, and then assigned them to one of four categories: exultant (high on positive experiences and low on negative experiences); beset (low on positive experiences and high on negative experiences); volatile (high on both kinds of experiences); and bland (low on both kinds of experiences).

The differences between the younger groups (students and newly-weds) and the older groups (middle-aged parents and pre-retirement people) were very marked. Half of the members of the older groups fell into the bland category, against less than 10 per cent of the younger groups. Thus, older people are more than five times as likely as younger people to experience few of the highs and lows of emotional life. In contrast, 44 per cent of the younger respondents were classified as volatile, against only 12 per cent of the older ones. The emotional picture that emerges is one that makes a lot of sense: as people get older, there is a progressive "flattening of affect".

What are the implications of these findings for the relationship between age and happiness? The most fundamental implication is that the relatively weak link between age and happiness conceals fairly profound effects of age on emotional experience. The decreased capacity to experience positive affect as one gets older tends to reduce happiness, but the decreased capacity to experience negative affect compensates for this. Since the decrease in positive affect tends to be greater than that in negative affect, there is some overall decline in happiness with increased age.

It might be argued that age-related changes in positive and negative emotional experiences rather go against the idea that personality is the major determinant of happiness. This would be true if personality remained the same. However, there is interesting evidence that personality tends to change somewhat during the course of life, with the typical changes being towards reduced extraversion and neuroticism or anxiety. Since extraversion is associated with positive affect and anxiety with negative affect, the changes in personality are exactly in line with the emotional changes. Thus, it may well be the changes in personality which produce the reduced emotional responsiveness of later life.

Older people are not as happy as younger ones, but it would be misleading to conclude that all of the advantages lie with youth. Satisfaction with life tends, if anything, to increase during most of the adult years. This satisfaction is based in part on the solid achievements (e. g., a contented family life, career success, and so on) that often characterize the middle years. The increased responsibilities that come with the passing of the years may limit the opportunities for pure happiness, but at the same time provide the basis for considerable satisfaction. However, the main reason why satisfaction with life is greatest among older people lies elsewhere. Older people usually have a relatively small discrepancy between aspiration and achievement, because their experiences of life enable them to be realistic about what can be achieved. In contrast, many young people have excessively optimistic dreams about the future, and the failure of most of these dreams is a potent source of dissatisfaction with life.

Job satisfaction

There is a general feeling that those in interesting and well-paid employment are happier than those doing routine and poorly paid jobs, and we will see shortly that there is some support for this viewpoint. However, there is a much larger difference in happiness between those who are employed (in whatever capacity) and those who are unemployed. For example, researchers in the United States found that only approximately 10 per cent of the unemployed described themselves as "very happy", in contrast to 30 per cent of the general population. Suicide rates tell the same story, since unemployed people are five times as likely as those with jobs to commit suicide.

It is hardly an earthshaking discovery that the unemployed are not especially happy, but what is less obvious is that unemployment has more impact on negative affect than on positive affect. In a recent British study, approximately 21 per cent of adults reported that they "felt very pleased with things all of the time yesterday", and the figure hardly differed between those in and out of work. On the other hand, while only 7 per cent of those in full-time employment said that they "felt unpleasant emotional strain all or most of the time yesterday", as many as 17 per cent of the unemployed fell into that category.

As people who retire often discover to their cost, work provides a number of hidden benefits. For example, it provides a structure to the week, it prevents life becoming aimless, it gives status and a sense of identity, and it usually provides several ready-made social contacts. In contrast, being out of work is very often perceived by the unemployed person as being a sign of failure: "If you can't find any work to do, you have the feeling that you're not human. You're out of place. You're so different from all the rest of the people around you that you think something is wrong with you."

Let us now turn to those who are in full-time employment. In the United States, 52 per cent are very satisfied with their jobs, 36 per cent are somewhat satisfied, and only 3 per cent are very dissatisfied. However, these figures may owe something to people "putting on a brave face", because a rather different picture emerged when people were asked whether they would work even if it were financially unnecessary to do so. Only 32 per cent said they would want to continue in their present job, which suggests that some people derive less genuine satisfaction from their jobs than they claim. However, nearly 70 per cent said that they would want to work at something even if financial necessity did not require them to do so. This would please Protestant reformers such as Calvin and Luther, who argued that a person's worth depends in large measure on the work he or she does, the so-called "Protestant work ethic".

What are the factors which determine job satisfaction and happiness? The most important factor is autonomy, which is the extent to which one's job provides independence and freedom from direct control. Other major factors are the extent to which various skills are involved in job performance, the amount of information which is available about job effectiveness, and the degree to which the job has a significant effect on the lives of other people.

This last factor has been emphasized by Eliot Jacques in his interesting analysis of the prestige associated with various jobs. According to him, people in prestigeful jobs make decisions which have very long-term consequences, whereas those who are not in prestigious jobs do not. Thus, for example, a surgeon's actions may affect the whole life of the person he is operating on, and the decisions of a Prime Minister or President can affect all of our lives over very long periods of time. In contrast, the decisions of a tea-boy or a road sweeper have minor and short-term consequences. When this principle of the time period over which decisions operate is applied to a wide range of jobs, it predicts amazingly well how prestigious each one is rated.

Another factor which influences job satisfaction is, of course, pay. However, it seems to do so largely in a negative fashion. In other words, poor pay can certainly cause job dissatisfaction, but there is less evidence that good pay actually does much to increase job satisfaction.

Cary Cooper at the University of Manchester has compared different jobs in terms of how stressful they are. Miners, the police, construction workers, journalists, civil pilots, and prison officers were found to have the most stressful jobs, whereas librarians, museum workers, nursery nurses, astronomers, vicars, and beauty therapists experienced the least stress at work. In terms of job satisfaction, it has been reported that the most satisfied people are university teachers (surely no longer true?), scientists, clergymen, and other professional people such as doctors and lawyers.

Job satisfaction is associated with life satisfaction. However, it could be that general satisfaction with life makes one more satisfied with one's job, rather than that having a satisfying job enhances general life satisfaction. There is some truth in both points of view. Finally, in case you remain unconvinced that how you feel about your job is important, just note that job satisfaction correlates 0.26 with length of life!

Socio-economic status

One of the major preoccupations of contemporary Western society is with their own and other people's social status and economic position. In the jargon of sociologists, we are obsessed by socio-economic status. In England, it is usually possible to identify someone's place in the social hierarchy purely on the basis of his or her accent, although the occupation, educational background, and family income all play a part. Much the same appears to be true of most other countries, no matter how vehemently the inhabitants of those countries claim to live in a "classless" society. Almost everywhere one looks, people are desperately attempting to better themselves in order to achieve higher socio-economic status. This willingness to participate in the so-called "rat race" indicates that there is a general feeling that improving one's social status is the royal road to happiness. Indeed, there are lots of people who regard socio-economic status and quality of life as virtually synonymous terms.

Is this striving for socio-economic status worthwhile? The answer is a qualified "yes". It is certainly true that those belonging to the professional and business classes tend to be happier than those of lower socio-economic status, but the law of diminishing returns applies to some extent. Those of intermediate socio-economic status are much happier than those of low socio-economic status, but the happiness gap between those of high and of intermediate socio-economic status is much less.

Further evidence that well-being and happiness depend on socio-economic status comes in a British study of employed men. Only four per cent of those in social classes I and II take time off each year because of mental disturbances. The corresponding figure for those in social class V is more than three times as high.

Why are those of high socio-economic status happier than the poor unfortunates cowering at the bottom of the social hierarchy? The first step in answering this question is to consider which of the two components of happiness (i.e., high positive affect and low negative affect) is more affected by socio-economic status. There are reasonable grounds for arguing that both components are affected. Those of high socio-economic status have greater control over their lives, and their affluence and social position provide them with numerous interesting options. We have already seen that those people with more control over their working lives are happier than those who work under regimented conditions. One might imagine that an enhanced ability to do what one wants should lead to greater positive affect. On the other hand, people who enjoy high socio-economic status are removed from at least some of the stresses and strains which beset the rest of us, and this should presumably reduce negative affect. Many people are worried that they will not have the money to pay for some unexpected expense such as a car repair bill or a leaky roof, but the upper middle classes have the comforting knowledge that they can solve such problems immediately by simply writing out a cheque.

In fact, while high socio-economic status individuals are both higher in positive affect and lower in negative affect than those of low status, the difference is three times greater for positive affect than it is for negative affect. The small effects of socio-economic status on negative affect may seem surprising in view of the greatly reduced money worries of individuals having high status, but they are not immune to most of the other stresses of life. Like everyone else, they may have poor health, an unhappy marriage, loved ones who die, lost career opportunities, and so on. However, they are rather less likely than low status persons to endure the miseries of divorce. The United States Bureau of the Census reported some years ago that men who earned under $3000 a year were approximately three times as likely as men earning over $8000 a year to be divorced during the first 20 years of their marriage.

In order to understand why middle-class people tend to enjoy more positive affect than working-class ones, Norman Bradburn initially embarked on a search for those aspects of behaviour which are especially associated with positive affect. He discovered two factors which were of comparable importance: sociability and novelty of experience. Sociability involves things such as making new friends, meeting new people, being active in social organizations, or chatting with friends on the phone. Novelty of experience simply involves doing things that you have not done before, or at least not for a long time (e.g., travelling to a particular country). Norman Bradburn hypothesized that the reason why positive affect was associated with socio-economic status was because individuals high in socio-economic status are more sociable and more inclined to seek novel experiences. The findings are exactly as predicted. Sixty-one per cent of high status men and 64 per cent of their wives are high in marriage sociability, but only 47 per cent of low status men and 34 per cent of their wives are high in marriage sociability. The strongest evidence of all is the finding that people of low socio-economic status, but high sociability and novelty of experience, experience more positive affect than those of high socio-economic status coupled with low sociability and novelty of experience.

We have now obtained a clear picture of why it is that high socio-economic status is conducive to greater happiness, but there are still one or two puzzles to consider. Why is it, for example, that working-class people don't increase their sociability and novelty of experience, and thus boost their levels of positive affect? Part of the answer may be that their relative poverty denies them some of the opportunities which are open to middle-class people. In addition, those of high status tend to obtain more positive affect from interacting with others than those of low status. High status people have much higher self-esteem than low status people, perhaps because they are treated in a more respectful and deferential way. In consequence, they find it rewarding to mix with other people.

While Norman Bradburn has made considerable headway in his attempt to explain the relationship between socio-economic status and happiness, there are limits to how much can be achieved by this approach. The reason is that socio-economic status really consists of a number of different factors all jumbled together. These factors include family income, occupation, educational background, and so on. We have already seen that the nature of one's job has a definite impact on the level of happiness. Additional information about the other determinants of happiness can be obtained by looking at some of these factors individually.

Income

Money has always been an emotive subject, and many different attitudes towards it have been expressed over the years. According to the First Epistle of Paul to Timothy, "The love of money is the root of all evil." In contrast, the Reverend Frederick J. Eikerenkoetter II, the head of the United Christian Evangelistic Association, typically addresses his congregation in the following way: "Now repeat after me! . . . I have a wonderful relationship with money . . . Money loves me . . . I see a mountain of money piling into my arms . . . I see myself on shopping sprees . . . taking fabulous vacations several times a year . . . with money to spare . . . Oh bless you, money, you're wonderful stuff!"

Despite varying views on the value of money, most people believe that those with high incomes tend to be happier with their lot than those with low incomes. However, the relationship is not as straightforward as one might imagine. Those with low incomes do, indeed, show a distinct tendency to be unhappy, but above a certain relatively modest level extra income typically has only a marginal effect on happiness. Norman Bradburn in the 1960s compared people of low income (under $2000 a year), average income (between $5000 and $6000), and high income ($10,000 a year or more). Those on average income were reasonably contented: 35 per cent of them said that they were "very happy", and only 9 per cent claimed to be "not too happy." The high earners showed a similar pattern of responses, although they were slightly more likely to be "very happy" (40 per cent) and a little less likely to be "not too happy" (5 per cent). A very different picture emerges when we examine the plight of the poorly paid. Only 18 per cent of them managed to be "very happy" in the face of financial hardship, and over one-third of them (36 per cent) were "not too happy."

What about those with extremely high incomes living in the style depicted in soap operas such as *Dallas* and *Dynasty*? Researchers in a recent American study investigated several aspects of happiness in a group of 49 very wealthy individuals, most of whom were earning over $10 million a year. These rich individuals were happy 77 per cent of the time on average, against 62 per cent of people chosen at random from the same areas. The same kind of difference emerged when both groups were asked about life satisfaction. Further probing revealed that the very rich experienced more positive affect and less negative affect than the random sample, but very high income decreased negative affect more than it increased positive affect.

Despite the fact that individuals earning millions of pounds a year tend to be happier than the rest of us, there is at least one fly in the ointment. The very rich, who are presumably in a position in which they do not need to concern themselves very much about money, nevertheless tend to have an obsessional concern with money. Compared to those with average incomes, the very rich are much more likely to agree with the statement, "I worry about my finances much of the time."

Why is high income associated with greater happiness? It is usually assumed that high income (coupled with the possession of a relatively interesting job) has a direct impact on the level of happiness. However, it is very likely that there are also indirect effects of happiness on income. For example, someone who is very unhappy because he or she is either anxious or depressed will probably make a bad impression at a job interview, and so will be unlikely to obtain the job. Even if someone suffering from a mood disorder does obtain a good job, they may subsequently lose it because their unhappy state prevents them from carrying out the job satisfactorily.

The fact that high incomes are more conducive to happiness than lower incomes may seem merely to confirm what we already knew via common sense. However, matters are not really as cut and dried as that. There has been much talk in the media about "executive stress", and it has often been argued that great psychological pressures are produced by a striving for material success. Anyone focussing on such executive stress might very well make the erroneous prediction that high wage-earners should be less happy than their less successful colleagues.

Even if executive stress does not cause individuals with high incomes to be unhappy, it is still possible that earning high wages produces significant stresses. Evidence for this could be obtained by considering separately the two components of happiness, viz., high positive affect and low negative affect. "Executive stress" would presumably manifest itself in increased negative affect rather than decreased positive affect. However, we have just seen that those with extremely high incomes are generally characterized by rather low levels of negative affect.

Perhaps the spectacular success of those earning millions of pounds a year prevents them from suffering much from executive stress. What about the effects of the normal range of income on positive and negative affect? Far and away the major effect of relatively high income is to increase positive affect, presumably because of the greater status, financial security, and ability to do what one wants that it confers. There is also a much more modest effect on negative affect, but it is in the direction of greater income being associated with reduced negative affect. Thus, there is really little or no truth in the notion that there is a trade-off between happiness and material success, nor is there any serious psychological price to be paid for financial success.

There are two main possible reasons why high income might enhance happiness. One possibility is that what is important is the absolute level of income. In other words, high income is beneficial because of the spending power which it gives the individual. An alternative possibility is that it is the relative level of income which matters. That is to say, those having a high income are happy mainly because they are doing relatively better than other people whom they know.

Of course, if we consider those with high income in our society, then their absolute and their relative levels of income are both high. However, we can decide whether it is the absolute or the relative level which is more important by comparing well off individuals at different times and in different countries. Such comparisons indicate very clearly that it is the relative level of income which is of primary importance. For example, those with high incomes nowadays are much better off than those with high incomes 20 or 30 years ago, but there is very little evidence that they are any happier. In similar fashion, the inhabitants of a wealthy country are not much happier than those living in a much poorer country such as India, and Europeans and inhabitants of Latin American countries differ little in their levels of happiness.

The unimportance of absolute levels of income was also demonstrated in a recent British study. Manual workers earning reasonably high wages were much more content with their pay than non-manual workers earning exactly the same amount. Presumably this is because the non-manual workers generally had higher initial expectations than the manual workers, and so were less likely to feel that they had achieved a satisfactory income.

Family life-cycle stage

Married people are generally somewhat happier than single or divorced people, and married people with children tend to be less happy than married people without children. The notion that children reduce their parents' level of happiness seems in some ways to be paradoxical. If the arrival of their first child reduced their happiness, why do most parents subsequently decide to have one or more additional children? It is also strange that, despite much evidence to the contrary, most parents still believe that having children has made them personally happier. Indeed, many parents would go further and whole-heartedly endorse the sentiments of the great philosopher Bertrand Russell: "I have found the happiness of parenthood greater than any other that I have experienced."

There is, in fact, a rather simple solution to the paradox that married couples continue to have children in spite of their happiness-reducing qualities. In essence, children have a magnifying effect on their parents' emotional states; that is to say, having children increases both positive and negative affect. Thus, there are great joys associated with the love that exists between parent and child, even if the overall level of parenal happiness suffers after the arrival of children in the home.

Why exactly do children reduce their parents' happiness level? In order to answer that question, it will be useful to consider the circumstances in which children produce the most marked reductions in marital happiness. A young child tends to produce more negative effects than an older child, especially when it is a pre-school child. The most stressful state of affairs, however, is when there are two or more pre-school children in the family. Thus, marital happiness is reduced in proportion to the minute-by-minute demands which children make on their parents. Attending to the needs of young children is a very demanding and time-consuming business, and produces major constraints on the activities of the primary caretaker. It is the substantial loss of control and freedom involved in bringing up young children which is the most important factor in lowering marital happiness.

The above analysis fits in well with the additional fact that it is usually the happiness level of mothers which suffers more than that of fathers from the presence of children. As feminists have pointed out repeatedly over recent years, the traditional family unit places particularly great stresses and limitations on the mother, whereas the father has more scope to maintain a separate existence outside the bosom of the family.

The size of the typical family has gone down dramatically during the course of the 20th century. Of course, the introduction of the pill and the increased determination of many women to have a family and to go out to work are important reasons for this change, but there is another reason which has been insufficiently appreciated. There have been subtle changes over the past one hundred years in the nature of marriage in Western society. The previous emphasis on marriage as the provider of status and financial security has now shifted to one on love and sexuality, and this may be a crucial change. Since status and financial security in the nineteenth century usually depended exclusively on the husband's job, whereas the wife was responsible for bringing up the children, it was entirely possible to achieve those major goals of marriage while having a large family. In contrast, achievement of the contemporary goals of love and sexuality requires that a married couple devote a considerable amount of time and attention to each other, and the presence of children tends to stand in the way of achieving those goals.

LEISURE

Happiness involves being satisfied with what one has in all of the main domains of life. Successful personal relationships and reasonable job satisfaction are of particular relevance, but it is also important to consider the amount of satisfaction obtained from leisure activities. Apart from anything else, leisure activities are likely to have an impact on happiness simply because people spend so much time away from work and other pressing commitments. An American study in which people kept a diary of their daily activities revealed that men had an average of 4 hours 46 minutes of free time per day, whereas employed women had an average of 4 hours 2 minutes.

What exactly is leisure? According to the social psychologist Michael Argyle, leisure "should be defined as those activities which people do simply because they want to, for their own sake, for fun, entertainment, self-improvement or for goals of their own choosing, but not for material gain." Most people seem to be rather satisfied with their own leisure activities as so defined. An American national survey indicated that 36.5 per cent were mostly satisfied with their leisure activities, 32.5 per cent were pleased, and 11 per cent were delighted.

The most popular leisure-time activity is watching television, which the average adult spends approximately 25 hours a week doing. There is no doubt that most people who spend a lot of time watching television derive much happiness from it. Another popular activity is drinking. The purpose of drinking was expressed succinctly by a legendary Chinaman:"Me no drinkee for drinkee, me drinkee for drunkee." This statement can be contrasted with the view of another anonymous philosopher: "If you want to be happy for a few hours, get drunk. If you want to be happy for a few years, get a wife. If you want to be happy for ever, get a garden."

A form of leisure activity which has been investigated in detail is the holiday. It has received a bad press of late, with distinguished academics like Professor Cary Cooper arguing that holidays often increase stress and reduce happiness rather than the opposite. It is true, of course, that holidays can impose various demands: the appropriate travel documents have to be obtained, accommodation has to be booked, mysterious illnesses can develop, foreign food may be unpalatable to some members of the party, and so on.

Despite the fact that there can be a stressful side to holidays, the evidence is indisputable that holidays generally increase the sum of human happiness. I recently collected information about the levels of positive and negative affect people had experienced on holiday and during a normal working period. While holiday brochures and advertisements tend to emphasize the way in which holidays can increase positive affect, it actually turned out that holidays did not increase positive affect, but they did produce a substantial reduction in negative affect. This is consistent with other evidence. In one study, it was found that holidays reduced the number of people complaining of tiredness from 34 per cent to 12 per cent, worry and anxiety from 27 per cent to 7 per cent, headaches from 21 per cent to 3 per cent, and loss of interest in sex from 12 per cent to 6 per cent.

Why do people choose certain leisure activities rather than others? The first attempt to answer that question systematically came from Engels, who was one of the founders of communism. He argued that work is very stressful and demanding for most people, and that people select their leisure activities because they provide a form of compensation. This viewpoint probably made more sense in the 19th century when Engels proposed it than it does now, because the number of people doing exceptionally stressful or unsatisfying jobs is much lower today. Nowadays compensation plays a major role in leisure for only 5 per cent of people, and a subsidiary role for a further 25 per cent.

Leisure can also be considered from the perspective of spillover theory, which is more or less the opposite of Engels's compensation theory. Many professional people such as academics and self-employed businessmen have no set hours of work. They often work at weekends and even on holiday, but more crucially it is often difficult to tell where work ends and leisure begins. The prime example of this so far as academics like myself are concerned is a conference. There is an element of work in that several hours a day are spent listening to talks and discussing academic matters with others, but there is also an element of social recreation. In addition, if a conference is held in an interesting place, there also tends to be some sightseeing.

The best example that comes to my mind of a conference which simultaneously fulfilled a number of work and leisure goals was a NATO conference held in Les Arcs in the French Alps. Approximately seven hours a day were spent in fascinating discussions devoted to the topic "Energetics and Human Information Processing", but every afternoon was free. This provided the opportunity to play golf and tennis, and to take splendid alpine walks. At the end of the day, everyone gathered for dinner at nine o'clock, and friendly discussions went on until at least midnight.

Despite the fact that my own working life conforms rather neatly to the spillover theory of leisure, I recognize that for most people it is just not true that leisure represents an extension of work activities. In fact, what is generally the case is that leisure is totally independent of work. It is independent not only in the sense of not spilling over from work, but also in the sense that it is generally very difficult to predict someone's leisure activities on the basis of the nature of their job. In other words, most people are neither so heavily involved in their work that they want it to carry over into their leisure time, nor so exhausted and stressed by it that they desperately seek for compensation in their leisure activities.

GENDER

It is generally accepted that women are far more emotional than men. As Alfred, Lord Tennyson expressed it:

"Man for the sword and for the needle she:
Man with the head and woman with the heart."

The same poet also gave voice to the related point of view that women tend to be more extreme than men:

"For men at most differ as Heaven and Earth,
But women, worst and best, as Heaven and Hell."

In spite of the fact that men and women are popularly believed to differ considerably in their emotional lives, there is actually only rather modest support for this belief. Men and women scarcely differ in terms of global happiness or satisfaction. However, the effects of ageing on happiness are somewhat different in the two sexes. Younger women tend to be a little happier than younger men, but older women are less happy than older men. The cross-over occurs at about the age of 45, and probably involves a number of factors. Women's overall level of happiness depends more than that of men on marital happiness, and marital happiness tends to decrease over the years. Men's overall level of happiness is importantly influenced by satisfaction at work, and many men move into more interesting, responsible, and well-paid jobs during their late thirties and early forties.

The most important emotional difference between men and women is that women tend to be more variable, in the sense that they experience more positive affect and more negative affect than men. So far as negative affect is concerned, an American study revealed that 37 per cent of women and 36 per cent of men worried much or all of the time, and that 25 per cent of women but only 12 per cent of men felt that they were about to have a nervous breakdown. The statistics of mental illness tell the same story. Women are 1.5 times as likely as men to suffer from anxiety neurosis, and twice as likely to suffer from depression.

There is an interesting sex difference in the reaction to being emotionally volatile, i.e., varying between high positive affect and high negative affect. Volatile women tend to be rather happy, whereas volatile men are not. In other words, men are more distressed than women by the ups and downs of emotional life. This may play a part in explaining why it is that women tend to be more volatile than men. What is also relevant is that women attach more importance than men to close emotional relationships, and so their moods are much affected by the successes and failures of such relationships. In contrast, men's emotional states are affected by job satisfaction, and this tends not to vary very much over time.

CONCLUSIONS

We have now considered the level of happiness in several different groups within society. The young have been compared with the old, those of high socio-economic status with those of low socio-economic status, those with young families with those with grown-up families, those with high income with those of low income, and so on. The consistent finding is that there are much larger differences in happiness within these groups than there are between them. In other words, membership of an apparently favoured group (e.g., young, high socio-economic status, married with no children) is no guarantee of happiness, nor does membership of an unfavoured group (e.g., old, low socio-economic status, divorced) necessarily condemn one to a life of misery.

The major reason why none of the demographic factors discussed in this chapter has a sizeable impact on happiness is because happiness is mainly determined by personality. A neurotic introvert belonging to a very favoured group in society will typically be less happy than a stable extravert belonging to an unfavoured group. Membership in any group is associated with various advantages and disadvantages; neurotic introverts focus on the disadvantages, whereas stable extraverts focus on the advantages. For example, the advantages of having a good job include being well paid and being respected by other people, and the disadvantages typically include having to work long hours and accepting much responsibility. In similar fashion, while high socio-economic status obviously confers a number of advantages, it also makes demands in terms of standards of behaviour which can be regarded as disadvantages.

There is a further, often overlooked, reason why most of the demographic variables have only modest effects on human happiness. There is a general tendency in Western society for people to live close to, and to be friendly with, other people who belong to the same broad groups. Those of high socio-economic status will usually live in the best residential areas, those with young children will be friendly with others having young children, and middle-aged people will usually have predominantly middle-aged people as their friends and acquaintances. The fact that like mixes with like reduces the tendency to compare oneself either favourably or unfavourably with other groups within society, and thus prevents us being very affected by demographic variables.

Suppose we had a society in which people were constantly exposed to the life-styles enjoyed by other groups in society. A middle-aged or old man living in a students' hall of residence might experience some unhappiness when he realized what active sex lives the students were leading. Similarly, someone with an average, modestly paid, job might well feel dissatisfied if he were continually talking to people doing much more prestigious and better paid jobs than him. In other words, demographic variables would have a fairly large effect on happiness if members of very different groups interacted frequently, but the actual organization of society prevents this from happening.

CHAPTER SIX

Why Happiness doesn't Last

A somewhat depressing lesson that we learn from life is that there is no guaranteed, sure-fire formula for happiness. Love, wealth, fame, good friends, or the ready availability of attractive sex partners can all provide us with happiness, but their beneficial effects all too often prove distressingly short-lived. There are undoubtedly some exceptions, based on religious faith or a very successful marriage, but the typical pattern is that a pleasant experience has less and less capacity to make us happy the more often it occurs. Thus, lovers of chocolate who go to work in a chocolate factory are actively encouraged to eat as many chocolates as they like. What nearly always happens is that their initial enthusiasm for consuming chocolates is later followed by a distaste for them. It is almost as if there is an inexorable law of diminishing returns in terms of the power of life's events to make us happy.

The first systematic attempt to clarify some of the factors at work here was carried out over a hundred years ago by a German physiologist called Weber. His simple (but quite revealing) experiment is one you could try out yourself. First of all, he prepared three bowls of water. In one bowl, the temperature of the water was 30°C, and in the other two it was 40°C and 20°C, respectively. What happened next was that the participant in the experiment put one hand in the bowl containing the warmest water, and the other other hand in the bowl with the coldest water for a couple of minutes. Immediately afterwards, he put both hands in the bowl which contained the water of intermediate temperature. While both hands were exposed to the same objective temperature, there was a surprisingly pronounced difference in the subjective experience. The water felt quite warm to the hand which had been in the cold water, but the very same water seemed rather cold to the hand which had been in the hot water!

Thus, the way in which we experience life's events depends in large measure on what we are used to. Our experiences are determined not only by what is currently happening to us, but also by what has happened in the past. These past experiences provide a kind of context or framework within which we evaluate what is happening to us now. A concrete example will help to make the point. A few years ago I spent some months in the pleasant surroundings of south Florida. When I arrived there in early January, I found the temperature (around 25°C) quite hot in contrast to the cold and gloomy English winter I had left behind. It came as a great surprise to find that the native population (who are used to a sub-tropical climate) was bemoaning the unseasonable coldness!

Of course, experiences of heat and cold are very different to feelings of happiness and unhappiness, and we cannot just assume that what is true of temperature judgements will necessarily apply to emotional experience. However, there do actually appear to be some important similarities. The so-called "law of hedonic contrast" has been put forward, according to which a pleasant occurrence will produce greater pleasure if it is immediately preceded by an unpleasant experience than by a pleasant one. This law of hedonic contrast seems to lend a certain psychological credibility to the old joke about someone justifying banging his head against a brick wall by claiming that he did it because it felt so good when he stopped.

The amount of happiness produced by any given event or experience, then, is not constant or absolute. Instead, happiness is relative, since it depends to a major extent on the context provided by previous experiences. It is also relative in that it depends on the immediate context as well. This notion is well-known to many restaurateurs. They appreciate that a rather ordinary and indifferent meal can often taste much better if it is consumed in a lavishly and attractively decorated restaurant. My wife and I have had personal experience of this particular context effect. There is a charming Indian restaurant near us which always seems to serve very appetizing food. Once or twice we have taken advantage of their take-away service. We were strangely disappointed in the quality of this food when eaten in the modest surroundings of our own home, not having realized sufficiently the important contribution of a restaurant's ambience to the enjoyment of a meal.

In fact, the happiness produced by an event can be affected in a number of ways by the immediate environmental context. There are cases (such as the restaurant example) in which the context seems to blend in with the event to form a single entity, but there are other situations in which the opposite happens, and the context provides a contrasting event against which the central event is compared. This kind of contrast effect was demonstrated in a study in which advertisements cut from a popular magazine were evaluated for pleasantness one at a time. Those advertisements that were rated averagely pleasant the first time around were rated a second time, but this time one of the most unpleasant advertisements was placed in the field of vision. This produced a contrast effect, in which the advertisements that had previously been rated as only averagely pleasant were now regarded as rather pleasant.

DOWNWARD COMPARISON AND SNOBBERY

There is a somewhat different kind of contrast effect which is widespread in everyday life. It involves people attempting to make themselves happier by comparing themselves and their achievements favourably to other people and their attainments, and it is usually known simply as snobbery. Snobs take great care to devalue the accomplishments of others in order that their own may seem even greater in comparison. If one can avoid feeling threatened by snobbery directed against oneself, then it can be quite amusing. Fairly recently, I went to a conference held in Vouliagmeni, which is a seaside resort near Athens in Greece. I naively imagined that a particularly snobbish woman I know would be at least modestly interested and impressed when I told her about it, but she immediately thought of an effective put-down. "Oh, you went to the mainland of Greece, did you?" she said. "We always find the Greek islands so very much more interesting."

The American psychologist Thomas Ashby Wills has considered snobbery and other related phenomena in some detail. He argued that snobbery is merely one illustration of a basic principle which he called the downward comparison principle: individuals can increase their happiness (or reduce their unhappiness) by means of comparison with a less fortunate other person or group. Of course, we know that it is not really the done thing to rejoice at the misfortune of others, and so we usually keep pretty quiet about it. An anecdote told by Ken Tynan, the writer and critic, illustrates the shock that occurs when someone breaks the taboo on giving voice to the downward comparison principle: "One night, Mandel told us in detail how he had been wounded. There was a long pause, and then Mel [Brooks] did something typical. He said, very slowly, 'I'm sure glad that happened to you, and not to me.' He wasn't being cruel, he was being honest. He just blurted out what we were all thinking but didn't dare to say."

There is at least one interesting exception to the general reluctance to appear to be rejoicing in the troubles of others, and that is humour. Most humour involves having fun at someone else's expense, and the target chosen to be ridiculed is generally already regarded as being of low status (e.g., minority racial or religious groups). In other words, humour often provides a kind of safety-valve. It allows people to use downward comparison to cheer themselves up without feeling guilty about it.

Under what conditions are people most inclined to engage in the process of downward comparison? People who are unhappy with themselves are most likely to compare themselves to less fortunate others. Someone who is threatened and made to feel inferior through a failure experience is especially likely to compare himself to other individuals who have been even less successful.

A very similar process can probably be invoked to account for the behaviour of the snob. As any amateur psychologist knows, a person who finds it necessary to keep on insisting that he is better than other people usually has severe doubts whether it is actually true. The motivation of the snob is to bolster his sagging ego and to reduce his unhappy mood state.

ADAPTATION LEVEL

An impressive attempt to make some sense out of the complexities of happiness has been based on the theories of the noted American psychologist Harry Helson. He attached considerable importance to the notion of "adaptation". Adaptation plays a prominent role in physiology. The celebrated physiologist Walter Cannon introduced the term "homeostasis" to refer to various physiological states in mammals (e.g., internal bodily temperature) which are maintained at fairly constant levels in spite of varying external conditions. Our internal bodily temperature is a good example of homeostasis.

To return to Harry Helson, his great insight was that adaptation processes occur at the psychological level as well as at the more primitive or basic physiological level. He used this as the basis for his adaptation-level theory. According to this theory, all current stimuli and events are interpreted and experienced in the light of the prevailing adaptation level. This adaptation level corresponds roughly to what we expect to happen on the basis of past experience, and represents a point of indifference or neutrality. In essence, what adaptation-level theory tells us is that the impact of any event on us depends heavily on the extent to which it deviates from what had been expected. If what actually does happen simply corresponds to expectation (or the adaptation level), then the psychological effects are negligible.

A concrete example of adaptation in operation was obtained in a study in which the fingers of one hand were dipped for several minutes into a jar of water maintained at a particular temperature. For all water temperatues between 10°C and 40°C, the water eventually ceased to produce any sensation of heat or cold at all. In other words, the adaptation level (or what was expected) had become essentially identical to the actual temperature of the water.

According to adaptation-level theory, what determines whether water is experienced as cold or hot is very straightforward: if the water is hotter than the adaptation level, then it is experienced as hot, but if it is colder than the adaptation level, then it appears to be cold. People who had become adapted to water at 10°C felt that water at 12°C was warm, whereas those who had adapted to 40°C water regarded 38°C as cold! These findings provide striking confirmation of the basic notion that how we experience events depends on what past experience has led us to expect.

What are the implications of adaptation-level theory for anyone interested in the pursuit of happiness? Most unfortunately, the theory suggests that happiness will usually be a rather transient phenomenon. The reason for this is that high levels of happiness are achievable only when the events that happen to us are much better than our expectations or adaptation level. Thus, paradoxically, happiness in the present is most attainable if our previous experiences have been sufficiently miserable and unhappy that we expect little of life. Problems start to accrue if everything in our personal, social, and work lives goes exceptionally well for us over a period of time. Of course, we enjoy our string of successes, but even while we are enjoying ourselves our adaptation level is creeping up all of the time. We expect more and more of life, and ever greater triumphs are needed to make us really happy.

Adaptation-level theory contains within it the notion that even the most enjoyable activities lose their savour with repetition due to an increasing adaptation level. The Irish writer George Bernard Shaw had something similar in mind when he argued that a perpetual holiday was a good working definition of hell. Of all the major sources of pleasure and happiness, sexual intercourse with someone one loves is one of the most important of all. According to adaptation-level theory, even this prized activity would become less enjoyable over time. This reduced enjoyment would be reflected in a so-called "honeymoon effect", in which high initial rates of sexual intercourse would be followed by lower rates.

Common sense obviously suggests that there is usually a reduction in sexual activity between two people as time passes, but that it is a rather gradual process. A systematic investigation of the honeymoon effect was carried out by placing advertisments in various publications such as *Penthouse* and *New Scientist* asking newly married couples who had kept a record of their rates of sexual intercourse to come forward. Rates of intercourse during the first year of marriage were looked at for those couples where the wife was a virgin at marriage and where she did not become pregnant during that year.

The most striking feature of the findings was that the excitement of sexual activity between two married people in love with each other seemed to diminish very quickly. On average, there were 17.5 acts of intercourse in the first month, but this figure was down to 16 in the second month, and 13 in the third. A year after marriage, there were only 8.5 sexual acts per month, which was slightly under half the initial rates. In other words, as adaptation-level theory argues, there is a law of diminishing returns due to rising expectations.

The "hedonic treadmill"

The sad fact that present happiness can serve to reduce the chances of future happiness has led some psychologists to talk about the "hedonic treadmill". In a treadmill, you always wind up where you started no matter how quickly you move. In life, happiness depends on life treating you better than you expected, but in the long run life is likely to treat you in pretty much the same way as you expected.

There are several commonplace illustrations of the way in which changing adaptation levels can reduce happiness. Most people accumulate more money as they get older, but typically they do not actually feel much better off. According to adaptation-level theory, the reason for this is that the kind of life-style they expect to have drifts almost imperceptibly upwards. Other familiar examples of changing adaptation levels can be found in sporting contexts. I enjoy playing golf, and find that a round of golf makes me a lot happier if I have played well than if I have played badly. However, my play has improved somewhat over the years, so that a score which would have delighted me 15 years ago would depress me now.

There are basically two major alternative strategies that can be used by someone who feels trapped on the hedonic treadmill. One approach is to attempt to fight the odds by seeking ever more extreme pleasures so that the present is always excitingly different from the past. The alternative approach is to follow the advice of Jesus Christ and of the Stoic philosophers, and simply step off the hedonic treadmill. These two extreme strategies can be illustrated by considering the lives of two famous people: Elvis Presley is a clear example of someone who followed the path of progressively greater pleasures, whereas Paul Getty exemplifies a rather more stoical approach to life.

The most striking advantage of focussing on such famous and wealthy people rather than on ordinary mortals is that fame and wealth give people the opportunity to live their lives in relative freedom from the constraints which life imposes on the rest of us. As a consequence, we know that Elvis Presley and Paul Getty behaved in ways which reflected their own choices rather than having behaviour forced on them by external pressures.

Elvis Presley. The somewhat grotesque life of Elvis Presley has been documented in great detail by Albert Goldman, and the following owes much to his excellent book. The key to Elvis's life-style is to be found in his favourite motto, which was simply, "Take it to the max!" He rapidly became bored with most things, but his wealth and fame gave him great scope for taking nearly everything to the "max" or extreme. Let us start with his attitude to games. Unlike most people, he was not content to have a quiet game of cards or darts. Instead, in his early twenties, Elvis acquired the habit of renting the Rainbow Rollerdrome in Memphis after it had closed to customers in the evening. He and the "Memphis Mafia" did not just roller-skate around the floor. What they usually did was to play a game called "War", of which Elvis was the proud inventor. The game was a simple one. There were two teams, and the object of the game was to knock over as many members of the opposing team as possible by any means. When that game lost its savour, there was the "Whip" game, in which up to 30 people held hands and circled the rink, with those on the outside moving much faster than those on the inside. An essential part of the set-up (not surprisingly!) was a first-aid team equipped with bandages, antiseptics, anaesthetics, and restoratives.

Elvis's idea of an exciting game was that it should be as dangerous as possible. Another game that was popular with him involved fireworks. Some of the Memphis Mafia would buy up to £15,000 worth of fireworks in today's money, including skyrockets, baby giants, firecrackers, and "nigger chasers", which moved rapidly and unpredictably until they exploded. Since the emphasis was on large and potentially lethal fireworks, everyone had to wear air force jump-suits plus gloves, helmets, and goggles. When they were all dressed up, they divided themselves into Blue and Red teams, and started hurling fireworks at the other team in a way which would not have been endorsed by the Royal Society for the Prevention of Accidents. Elvis was left with a big scar on his neck from one firework, and one of his friends nearly lost an eye.

As you might have guessed, Elvis was no gourmet when it came to food. Following his own instructions to "take it to the max", he ballooned up to a weight of 18 stone and 3 pounds at the time of his death. In his late thirties, he developed a taste for special sandwiches sold at the Colorado Mine Company restaurant in Denver. These sandwiches, which cost the staggering sum of over £60 in today's money, consisted of a whole loaf of French bread sliced twice all the way from one end of the loaf to the other, stuffed full of peanut butter, jam, and a pound of bacon. On the first of February 1976, Elvis and his friends decided they would like some of these sandwiches. Immediately they all flew off to Denver from Memphis, with the return trip plus sandwiches costing approximately £20,000.

Elvis's attempts to make himself happy by taking everything to extremes are perhaps clearest with respect to his use of drugs. Up until the end of his Army career, Elvis seems to have been relatively sparing in his use of drugs. His main drugs at that time were simple pep pills such as benzedrine and amphetamine. When he was in his thirties, Elvis was taking a bewildering mixture of "uppers" and "downers". He would often take uppers to prepare himself for a public appearance, followed by downers afterwards to calm him down. At this time, he made something of a specialist study of drugs. His favourite book became *The Physician's Desk Reference*, which is a bulky tome describing the properties of virtually every pill known to man. When Elvis was asked one day which drug he preferred, he replied: "I've tried them all and Dilaudid is best." Dilaudid is an extremely powerful opiate which is approximately two-and-a-half times as strong as heroin.

When Elvis's body was examined by Dr. Norman Weissman after his early death at the age of 42, it contained no fewer than 12 different sorts of pills and drugs: morphine, quaalude, demerol, aventyl, codeine, valium, valmid, placidyl, amytal, nembutal, carbrital, and sinutab. What was staggering was not only the variety of substances that Elvis had taken, but also the amounts. Just considering the codeine, Elvis had a concentration of that drug some ten times higher than what is generally regarded as the toxic level.

Elvis's desperate attempts to keep himself happy by taking ordinary pleasures to absurd lengths can also be seen in his attitude towards money. It is difficult to establish precise figures, but Elvis during his lifetime probably earned something in excess of $100 million. However, despite his enormous earning power, Elvis was almost broke towards the end of his life. We have already seen that his use of drugs was a heavy drain on his resources, and impulsive gestures like flying across America in pursuit of special sandwiches were also expensive. Perhaps the most characteristic feature of Elvis's spending patterns was that he was never satisfied with one of anything. Thus, when he decided that he had to have a plane, he did not content himself with just a single plane, but instead went out and bought himself four multi-engined planes. One evening in Memphis when he wanted a car, he simply went out and bought 14 brand-new Cadillacs. Seeing an old Negress looking with amazement at this fleet of gleaming new cars, Elvis casually invited her to pick one for herself.

The most celebrated examples of Elvis's extreme and extravagant actions concern his dealings with girls. During his younger days, he was surprisingly inhibited and conventional with girls, but matters changed considerably when he came out of the United States Army in 1960. Shortly afterwards, he moved into a doughnut-shaped house in Bel Air which had previously belonged to the Shah of Iran, and the parties began. The parties were a little unusual in that there would be about 40 or 50 girls and only seven or eight men. The girls were recruited by Elvis's "Guys", with those selected being pretty, no older than eighteen, no taller than five foot two, and weighing no more than 110 pounds. Starting time for the parties, which were held virtually every night, was 10 o'clock. They were held in the den, with loud rock music coming from a jukebox filled with some of Elvis's favourite records. At about two in the morning, Elvis would select the "pick of the litter" in the form of two or three of the prettiest girls, and retreat with them into the master bedroom. There the usual arrangement was that the girls would strip down to their panties and wrestle with each other. This would not normally be followed by sexual intercourse, but by various other sexual activities such as fellatio.

Technology came to Elvis's aid a few years later when the unchanging routine of his parties was beginning to pall. He managed to get hold of the first Sony videotape machine designed for home use. This allowed him to become a film-maker, specializing in bedroom scenes of beautiful young women wrestling fiercely with each other and simulating lesbian sex. In later years, these films were made more exciting when Elvis began to make use of a beautiful lesbian who worked at the Sahara Tahoe Hotel in Las Vegas. Her prized skill was the ability to arouse other girls sexually, and to make them less self-conscious in front of the camera.

The parties in the final phase of Elvis's life became nothing more nor less than orgies. Girls would be brought to his house in Palm Springs, and everyone would start smoking hash early in the evening. When everybody was stoned, they would all undress and jump into the swimming pool. Afterwards the girls would be dragged off to the various bedrooms which were conveniently close to the pool. Elvis would not normally take part directly in the orgy, but rather would get down to the serious business of filming young girls.

The life of Elvis Presley illustrates vividly the fallacy in the common belief that the more you have of something you enjoy, the happier you will be. The basic approach taken by Elvis was that if one party, one girl, one Cadillac, or one drug made him happy, then vast quantities of parties, girls, and so on, would make him much happier. Unfortunately, you cannot escape from the hedonic treadmill that easily. When you have become used every week to seven parties and a dozen or more beautiful girls frolicking in your bed, what can you possibly do for an encore? The fact that there is no good answer to that question led Elvis to unhappiness, despair, and an early grave.

Paul Getty.   Paul Getty's life reveals precisely the opposite strategy of pursuing happiness. Instead of spending money lavishly in the attempt to make himself happy, Getty was almost totally unaffected by his phenomenal wealth. For example, he would sometimes queue on the pavement outside a restaurant in order to avoid having to pay the supplement for the orchestra. He explained his reasons as follows: "If you know the cover charge in a certain restaurant is off at 10 o'clock and it's a substantial charge, would you rather go in and maybe spend ten or fifteen dollars for the sake of a few minutes? That would be splashing money around and showing off." This may sound like good sense, but think of the impact of the lost ten or fifteen dollars on a fortune of approximately one thousand million dollars!

Not surprisingly, Getty was by no means convinced that money could buy happiness or a good time. He claimed that some of the most enjoyable times he could remember had involved the virtually free pastime of surfboarding. Indeed, in some ways he regarded wealth as a burden rather than a source of pleasure. As he pointed out to the television interviewer Alan Whicker: "There is a lot to be said for the ordinary man in the street. He has many advantages. Large financial responsibilities are not the key to cheerfulness."

Why was Paul Getty so morose and generally unhappy with his life? Part of the answer probably lies in the fact that his father was a millionaire, and so he spent most of his life in complete financial security. According to adaptation-level theory, since Getty expected to be able to buy whatever he wanted from an early age, his spending power would gradually lose its ability to make him happy. Another important part of the answer stems from Getty's personality. As I stressed in Chapter Two, the most important determinant of happiness is undoubtedly personality. The fact that the wealthiest man in the world could be so dour and miserable provides striking support for this point of view. Getty himself bemoaned his deficiencies of character: "I have always wished I had a better personality, that I could entertain people better, be a better conversationalist. I have always worried I might be a little on the dull side."

The lives led by Elvis Presley and by Paul Getty were obviously very different, but there are some important similarities. Although both men were extremely wealthy and famous, they still found it difficult to escape from the inexorable workings of the hedonic treadmill. Elvis Presley attempted to cheat the hedonic treadmill by running faster and faster. As the years went by, he had more girls, more drugs, more food, and more of just about everything else. All this increased consumption achieved was to raise his adaptation level, so that what he expected from life went up and up. It is tempting to believe that it was his growing realization that he couldn't run quickly enough to make any progress on the hedonic treadmill that led to Elvis's ultimate self-destruction.

Paul Getty exemplifies the resigned approach to the hedonic treadmill. Whereas Elvis Presley struggled with increasing desperation to make himself happier, Paul Getty adopted a much more passive approach. It was as if he said to himself: "There is nothing much I can do to make myself happier, so I am not even going to try." As his characteristically gloomy expression indicated, stepping off the hedonic treadmill altogether is not really the way to achieve lasting happiness.

Winning a fortune

Despite the example of Paul Getty, most people believe that being wealthy would make them happier. Even a little extra money would apparently have a cheering effect. Joyce Brothers, the television psychologist, asked Americans whether they would be happier if they were suddenly to become 25 per cent better off financially. An overwhelming majority said that they would.

It is interesting to note that adaptation-level theory makes a different prediction to that following from a common sense approach. According to adaptation-level theory, extreme good fortune such as winning a huge amount of money on the football pools should affect happiness relatively little in the long run. At the most general level, the reasoning behind this prediction is that happiness stems from experiences which are above the current adaptation level or point of indifference. Since adaptation level is constantly changing as a result of our experiences, the adaptation level of the very fortunate should go up as they come to expect life to treat them very well. Objectively, their lives should be better in some sense, but subjectively their increased expectations prevent them from feeling any happier.

Some fascinating insights into the impact of sudden wealth on ordinary British people were chronicled by sociologists Stephen Smith and Peter Razzell. They interviewed 88 people who had won at least £75,000 at 1957 money values on the football pools, which is equivalent to approximately one million pounds in today's money. A popular stereotype of pools winners is that they indulge in an orgy of spending, and this notion was confirmed by the case of Vivian Nicholson, a pools winner whose motto was "spend, spend, spend." In fact, one of the most striking findings was that sudden wealth typically has very modest effects on most people's lives. Of course, pools winners tend to move to a better house and to buy a better car, but only a tiny proportion of them become reckless with money. The general flavour of the reaction to winning a fortune is conveyed in one man's description of his thoughts after winning: "I think all people imagine these things. I certainly did, you know—what it would be like when you had a fantastic amount of money—but you certainly didn't plan seriously. You know you'd sort of think, if I won the Pools it's straight away a Rolls Royce and a trip round the world. Well actually it didn't come out like that. Soon as I knew we'd won it we started sitting down and talking and all the sort of fairy tale dreams like go out of the window when you realise it's there."

This man's wife confirmed the view that their substantial win had produced only relatively modest effects on their lives. According to her "The mortgage was the main thing, and little luxuries we'd never been able to have: a washer, save one doing it by hand, different little things like that."

Apart from property, cars, and household articles, most of the money won by pools winners tends to be invested. Seventy-seven per cent of the pools winners invested most of their win, usually in stocks and shares, Building Societies, or Local Government bonds. The overall picture is one in which the money which had been won was handled in a very conservative and careful fashion. There was not even much of a tendency to splash out on expensive holidays in exotic places. Pools winners were no more likely than non-winners to have had a holiday during the twelve months before being interviewed, and they were not more likely to have gone abroad for their holidays. In fact, the holiday places where you are most likely to bump into pools winners are the respectable English resorts of Bournemouth and Scarborough! Over half of the pools winners agreed that winning hadn't changed their way of life. David Llewellyn, who was the son of a Welsh miner, put it like this: "I don't think I have changed as a result of the win. I still go to the same places; and the few real friends that I had, I still have—thank God." Another winner, John Sellens, echoed this sentiment: "I haven't changed, ask any of the lads—they'll tell you. It's silly to change really, it don't make any difference to me, it hasn't made a scrap of difference, because I still go out with the same people."

While the effects of large pools wins seem rather modest, there are clearly some advantages and disadvantages that are likely to be experienced. On the positive side, the ability to buy whatever one wants is obviously desirable, and some winners took advantage of their win to leave their jobs and set up their own businesses. On the negative side, winning the pools can be a very disruptive event. Most pools winners give up their work almost immediately. Even if they want to keep working, their work-mates usually put pressure on them to let someone more in need of money have their job. As a result, pools winners often become bored and turn to drink. Richard Taylor, who won £312,000, reacted to winning in the following unfortunate way: "I was an alcoholic, I went to hospital with it, it crippled me, really crippled me. For about two and a half years I was a total drunk from morning to night. I used to get up in the morning and drink about half a pint of brandy for breakfast, straight out of the cup! ... I used to drink through boredom, bloody boredom that's all, and misery."

Winning the pools can also be disruptive in terms of social identity. Conflict is produced by the frequent discrepancy between a working-class existence prior to the win and the ability to live in a very comfortable middle-class style afterwards. Many of the winners were aware of this problem, and were unsure which social class they belonged to. Over half of non-winners were definite about their social class, against only 28 per cent of the pools winners.

Another problem with winning the pools is that it can pose a threat to the stability of one's marriage. Smith and Razzell calculated that pools winners were more than three times as likely as non-winners to separate or divorce. However, these figures may well exaggerate the adverse effects of winning on the marital relationship. In some cases, marriages that were essentially dead anyway were terminated by winners when they acquired the financial resources to be able to afford a divorce.

A final problem faced by many pools winners is the envy that relatives, friends, and work-mates may display. However, this problem is less widespread than one might have guessed. Only eight per cent of the winners said that their relatives' reactions had been negative, with a further eleven per cent experiencing mixed reactions from their relatives.

Clearly the experiences of the pools winners varied considerably from individual to individual. However, as Smith and Razzell pointed out, sudden wealth typically has an "amplification effect", that is to say, it amplifies or exaggerates certain aspects of behaviour that were already present. For example, a very shy and retiring winner stopped work after his win, and so had even fewer social contacts than before. A winner who was fond of practical jokes began to carry out more elaborate ones after his win.

He arranged that someone he had argued with should wake up to discover a dead horse in the middle of his garden.

Stephen Smith and Peter Razzell considered finally the key question of whether the money won on the pools had made the winners happier. Even though most of the other evidence which they collected seemed to indicate that the effects of the win were rather modest, Smith and Razzell found that 77 per cent of the winners claimed that they were happier as a result of their win. However, it is probable that some of the winners claimed to be happier because they thought they ought to be rather than because they actually were. The reason for arguing this is that some of them said things during their interview which belied their claims to enhanced happiness.

The impact of sudden wealth on happiness was also looked at by Philip Brickman and his colleagues at Northwestern University in the United States. They selected recent major winners of the Illinois State Lottery, nearly all of whom had won at least one hundred thousand dollars, and one-third of whom had won one million dollars. The views of these lottery winners mirrored those of the British pools winners in many ways. They mentioned a number of changes in their lives (e.g., financial security, greater leisure time), but nevertheless only 23 per cent of them felt that their general life-style had altered.

The lottery winners were then asked about their level of happiness at three different stages of their lives: before winning the lottery; the present post-win period; and two years in the future. Precisely as predicted by adaptation-level theory, the lottery winners did not feel any happier after their big win than before it, and they did not expect to be happier in two years' time. Moreover, winning a huge amount of money failed to make the lottery winners any happier than people who had not enjoyed such good fortune.

These findings are very relevant to the long-standing controversy between the growing army of materialists on the one hand, and religious authorities and moralists on the other hand. The latter group of anti-materialists seem to have won a crushing victory with these findings, since even a huge increase in personal wealth failed almost totally to increase happiness or enjoyment of life. The findings are even more striking in that they were obtained in a society which is usually regarded as being very materialistic.

The notion that money has a very limited ability to make people happier can be illustrated further by considering the effects of increasing affluence in Western society. In the United States of America, the average income in 1970 was approximately 60 per cent higher than in the late 1940s, after taking inflation and tax rates fully into account. However, this substantial increase in buying power led to no commensurate increase in happiness; indeed, the average level of happiness did not increase at all.

According to adaptation-level theory, the euphoria of winning a fortune in a lottery should increase the winner's adaptation level and expectations, and thus make the pleasurable events of everyday life seem less enjoyable than they were before. Philip Brickman explored this possibility. He asked the lottery winners how pleasant they found several activities or events such as watching television, talking with a friend, hearing a funny joke, and reading a magazine. The lottery winners derived much less pleasure from these activities than did non-winners.

All in all, the message that emerges from investigating those who have become wealthy overnight is that money cannot buy happiness. Thus, there is some psychological validity in stories such as those about the Sorcerer's Apprentice, King Midas, or Doctor Faustus, all of which provide potent warnings of the dangers associated with our most cherished dreams coming true. As the great Irish dramatist George Bernard Shaw pithily expressed it: "There are two tragedies in life. One is not to get your heart's desire. The other is to get it."

Misfortune and happiness

Philip Brickman devised a very stringent test of adaptation-level theory. He selected people who had experienced great misfortune, namely, recent accident victims. Two-thirds were quadriplegics having practically no use of their arms and legs, and the remainder were paraplegics having paralysis of the legs and part of all of the trunk. According to adaptation-level theory, their great ill luck should make them very unhappy at first, but subsequently their adaptation level should decrease to take account of their bad fortune. As a result, their reduced expectations should serve the useful purpose of allowing them to derive much pleasure from life's ordinary activities. This notion that people adjust successfully to adverse circumstances is summed up in the Arab proverb, "Throw a man into the sea, and he will become a fish."

What were the actual effects on the happiness of these people of their crippling accidents? They were still able to enjoy many things in life, since the pleasure they obtained from everyday activities (e.g., talking with a friend) did not differ from that of ordinary people. In terms of general happiness, the accident victims reported having been happier than ordinary people before their accident, and they expected to be at least as happy as other people in two years' time. The only exception to this pattern of surprisingly great enjoyment of life by the recently crippled (within the previous year in all cases) was the evaluation of present happiness, where their ratings were lower than those of ordinary people. Even here, the quadriplegics and paraplegics rated their present happiness above the midpoint of the scale, and they were clearly not in the state of despair and chronic unhappiness that might reasonably have been expected.

While the findings from accident victims broadly support adaptation-level theory, they do not do so in every particular. For example, the traumatic effects of the accident should have reduced adaptation level and expectations so that life's ordinary events seemed more pleasurable than they did to other people, but this did not happen. Instead, the quadriplegics and paraplegics claimed that they had enjoyed those events much more than most people prior to their accident. This nostalgia effect may have reduced their enjoyment of their post-accident lives.

Richard Schulz and Susan Decker looked at the long-term effects of physical disability. They considered the happiness levels in paraplegic and quadriplegic individuals approximately 20 years after the injury occurred. They reported somewhat lower positive affect than the general population, but not increased negative affect. As a consequence, their average level of well-being or satisfaction with life was only slightly lower than that of the general population. Indeed, those among the physically disabled group who had good social support from family and friends were as happy as ordinary individuals.

As might be expected by adaptation-level theory, these quadriplegics and paraplegics even managed to perceive some advantages in having been crippled. Many of them argued that brain is more important than brawn, and that their accident had led to personal growth, increased patience and tolerance, and an increased awareness of self.

The happiness and contentment of blind people have also been investigated. Vision is far and away the most important of the sense modalities, since we use it in virtually all of our work and leisure activities. Even such simple activities as walking down the street or reading a book become difficult and laborious in the absence of sight. However, despite the huge restrictions imposed by blindness, blind people have generally been found to be as happy as their sighted counterparts.

We have just seen that most people seem to cope remarkably well with the constraints imposed on their lives by severe physical disabilities. Even more amazing coping skills were demonstrated by many of those incarcerated in Nazi concentration camps during the Second World War. The psychologist Bruno Bettelheim was in the camp at Dachau, and has written movingly of his experiences there. When he arrived at Dachau and could not eat the awful food, he received the following lesson in survival from one of the prisoners who had already been there for some time: "Make up your mind: do you want to live or do you want to die. If you don't want to live, don't eat the stuff. But if you want to live, there's only one way: make up your mind to eat whenever and whatever you can, never mind how disgusting. Whenever you have a chance, defecate, so you'll be sure your body works. And whenever you have a minute, don't blabber, read by yourself or flop down and sleep."

As a psychologist, Bettelheim was well aware that the advice he had been given was sound and full of psychological wisdom. In his own words: "What [the advice] implied was the necessity, for survival, to carve out, against the greatest of odds, some areas of freedom of action and thought, however insignificant . . . To have some small token experiences of being active and passive, each on one's own, and in mind as well as in body—this, much more than the utility of any one such activity, was what enabled me and others like me to survive."

Similar impressive evidence of human ability to adapt to the most adverse circumstances has been described by the Russian writer, Alexander Solzhenitsyn. He spent eight long years in various Siberian labour camps. His experiences in a camp in the Karaganda region of northern Kazakhstan formed the basis for his celebrated novel, *One Day in the Life of Ivan Denisovich*. While one might imagine that life in a Siberian labour camp would be a hell on earth, the message of the book is actually uplifting. The hero of the book, Ivan Denisovich Shukhov, is by no means unhappy, and the reasons can be seen if we consider his evaluation of the day in his life described in the book: "Shukhov went to sleep fully content. He'd had many strokes of luck that day: they hadn't put him in the cells, they hadn't sent the team to the settlement; he'd pinched a bowl of kasha at dinner; the team-leader had fixed the rates well; he'd built a wall and enjoyed doing it; he'd smuggled that bit of hacksaw-blade through; he'd earned something from Tsezar in the evening; he'd bought that tobacco. And he hadn't fallen ill. He'd got over it. A day without a dark cloud. Almost a happy day."

Ivan Denisovich Shukhov is "almost happy" because his experiences in the labour camp have made him change his adaptation level so much that things such as not falling ill and buying some tobacco are good reasons for feeling "fully content" with life. It is difficult to imagine that most people would feel that they had had a good day simply because they were still in good health and had been able to buy tobacco! Thus, Solzhenitsyn's account of life in a Siberian labour camp provides a striking endorsement of adaptation-level theory.

Great misfortune of various kinds has been found to cause people to change their adaptation level or expectations so that they are better able to cope with, and to enjoy, their post-misfortune lives. However, it is obviously true that there are limits to the extent to which people can adapt to adversity. For example, mothers of handicapped children find it very difficult to cope, and report rather low levels of happiness as a result.

BEYOND ADAPTATION LEVEL

The simple notion that good and bad events gradually lose their power to produce an emotional reaction because of the adaptation process has proved very successful in accounting for many of the puzzling phenomena associated with happiness. However, it needs to be extended to account for individual differences in happiness level. If adaptation makes all events lose their power to affect us emotionally, then why do people with different personalities vary so much in their levels of happiness? The obvious answer is that our emotional reactions to events are determined only in part by the adaptation levels we have formed on the basis of past experience. Alternatively, individuals may differ in the extent to which their emotional reactions to events are influenced by adaptation levels rather than by their direct experience of the events themselves.

The personality dimension of introversion-extraversion may be particularly important here. Introverts (literally people who are "turned inwards") seem to respond emotionally by mentally comparing what is happening to them against what has happened in the past. Extraverts (people who are "turned outwards") respond more directly to current events and are less inclined to compare the present with the past. Thus, if an introvert went to a dinner party, he might say to himself, "This is quite a good dinner party, but since I can remember some better dinner parties, it is not really all that enjoyable." In contrast, an extravert might think simply, "This is quite a good dinner party, and I'm certainly going to enjoy myself." Thus, the emotional reactions of extraverts are less shackled and inhibited than those of introverts by memories of past experiences. This allows extraverts to experience more happiness than introverts, and so to escape to some extent from the "hedonic treadmill" described earlier in the chapter.

SOCIETY AND THE HEDONIC TREADMILL

Adaptation-level theory may be of relevance to broader issues relating to the happiness and contentment of an entire society. A key problem is that we want people to be happy, but making them happy raises their expectations and may make it harder for them to be happy in future (i.e., the hedonic treadmill).

What can be done to resolve the problems associated with the hedonic treadmill? One partial answer is to try to prevent particularly pleasurable events from affecting the adaptation level. One way in which this can be achieved is by separating off those events from normal life so that they do not affect our everyday expectations. In our society, the prime example of such an event is Christmas, which is set aside as a period of special indulgence. We expect to eat and drink much more than usual, to spend more money, and to devote ourselves wholeheartedly to the task of enjoying ourselves in a series of pleasant social activities. This would normally raise the adaptation level or our expectations for the future, but it does not do so to any great extent because it is so clearly different from everyday life.

The same reasoning applies to holidays. One of the reasons why we go abroad or to other parts of the country for our holidays is because this emphasizes the notion that holidays are somehow special and different from our everyday lives. Since they are so different, they do not have much effect on our expectations when we return home. This could explain why having holidays at home can be strangely unsatisfying. We become used to all of the pleasant features of holidays (e.g., having the family together, relaxing, going on trips), but we then find it difficult to adjust to having to return to a more demanding and stressful style of life in the same surroundings.

According to adaptation-level theory, one of the simplest ways of increasing the pleasure we derive from some activity is to attempt to reduce the adaptation level beforehand. This approach is associated with the world's major religious organizations, most of which advocate periods of abstinence. For example, the Islamic tradition of Ramadan involves complete fasting during the hours of daylight throughout the ninth month of the Moslem year. The abstinence itself may not be pleasurable, but it serves the useful function of whetting the appetite for the resumption of normal activities.

Our adaptation level and expectations depend in part on our knowledge of other people and their experiences. Thus, if someone living near you is earning much more than you are despite being no more intelligent or hard-working than you are, then you tend to feel that you deserve to be equally well rewarded. In other words, your adaptation level goes up and you begin to feel more discontented than before with your lot.

There are two major ways in which society can sort out the problems which can arise from comparisons that people make with other people. One way is to have an unequal society, but to arrange matters so that people tend not to compare themselves directly with those much more powerful and wealthy than themselves. Centuries ago, society was organized in a rigid hierarchical fashion, and positions within that hierarchy were determined almost entirely by parentage. As a result, while a servant might have been well acquainted with his master's luxurious and self-indulgent life-style, the perceived differences between them tended to prevent him from comparing himself with his master. Thus, an apparently unjust system was maintained because it was perceived as being reasonably fair and did not produce much unhappiness.

The other solution is the utopian notion of a perfectly equal society. While many great philosophers and other thinkers have advocated that kind of society, it is an unachievable goal. Suppose that everyone within a society received the same amount of money for the work they did. This would be equality of a kind, but there would still be some people who did work that was boring or dangerous. Of course, we could modify the system so that there was a trade-off between the interest level of the job and the financial rewards associated with it, but it is most unlikely that there would be universal agreement about the precise form of the trade-off.

The general problem with an equal society is that making people equal is often regarded as unfair. A 50-year-old man in a responsible position with great skills and experience should be more highly paid than a 20-year-old man who is just embarking on his career—which flies in the face of equality. If account were to be taken of age and responsibility, there is the tricky question of the extent to which wages should be affected by these factors.

In our present Western society, we are in danger of creating an unhappy society that falls between two stools. On the one hand, we have created a very unequal society in which most of the wealth is concentrated in rather few hands. In Britain, for example, just one per cent of the population owns almost one-third of all the wealth. While this state of affairs would probably be regarded as somewhat immoral, it might nevertheless not be conducive to unhappiness if there were a general acceptance that some people were much more deserving than others of wealth and privilege. However, the media and especially television tell us that we are as deserving as the next person, and advertisements persuade us that we should have a range of luxury goods previously affordable only by the wealthy few.

The media have not only encouraged us to compare ourselves with those further up the social and financial scales than we are, they have also supplied us with far more detailed information than was available before about the life-styles of those more affluent than ourselves. We now know how much the average doctor and lawyer earn, we have seen pictures of the homes of the wealthy in magazines, and we even know something of the sex lives of famous people. The media have thus enabled us to see exactly what pleasures and privileges denied to us are enjoyed by other people. This naturally produces a certain amount of resentment and unhappiness, fuelled by the so-called "revolution of rising expectations."

Social engineers, politicians, sociologists, and philosophers have all pondered whether there are any ways in which an entire society can be made happier and more contented. The capitalist answer of expanding production so that the population becomes wealthier has not really succeeded in promoting happiness. Indeed, if anything levels of happiness have gone down despite the massive increase in spending power over the last 40 years. The reason is clear within the context of adaptation-level theory: people respond to increased prosperity by expecting it to increase, and these rising expectations diminish the happiness that prosperity would otherwise have produced.

In view of our tendency to compare ourselves with others, coupled with the immense amount of knowledge of other people provided by the media, there is much to be said for a more egalitarian society. Apart from the obvious moral advantages, an egalitarian society would limit the extent to which expectations race ahead of reality and thus cause discontentment. Of course, there are problems with establishing a fair and just society, and not everyone would agree on exactly what would constitute such a society. However, there is something tragically unfair about the present state of affairs in America, in which there are almost one million millionaires but queues in front of the soup kitchens, and a fairer society could easily be created. Common sense might well have suggested a similar solution to the problem of increasing society's happiness, but it is reassuring to discover that the solution accords so well with the important psychological insights of Harry Helson.

CHAPTER SEVEN

How to be Happy

Throughout human history until recently the great majority of people were very preoccupied with the effort of making sure that they and their children had somewhere suitable to live and enough food to eat. As a consequence of such pressing concerns, there was precious little time left over for the self-indulgent luxury of worrying about such relative trivia as the ways in which personal happiness might be maximized. Even in Victorian times, many people had to go out to work every single day of the year with the exception of Christmas Day.

Life for most people in Western society is no longer "nasty, brutish, and short." Someone who goes out to work for 40 hours a week, and who sleeps eight hours a night, still has approximately 70 hours a week available for other activities. It is at least in part because of the great growth in leisure time that there is an increasing focus on happiness as a major goal in life. There is a general feeling that everyone has a right to be happy, and that something should be done about it if someone is not happy with his or her life. This increased emphasis on happiness is reflected by the rapidly escalating number of people whose jobs revolve around making other people happier or at least less unhappy. Nowadays we take it for granted that anyone who is unhappy can seek guidance from popular books, social workers, marriage guidance counsellors, psychotherapists, and psychiatrists if they want to improve the quality of their lives.

While many of the caring professions have made very valuable contributions to the sum of human happiness, it is paradoxical for someone to expect a relative stranger to make him or her happier. After all, each of us is presumably a great expert on our own emotional states, and we know extremely well from a life-time of experience what makes us happy or unhappy. Is it not unreasonable to anticipate that another person who cannot possibly know us as well as we know ourselves can be in a position to re-direct our lives in happier and more fruitful directions?

In fact, the paradox is apparent rather than real. People usually have rather subjective and biased opinions about themselves, whereas an expert outsider is likely to be objective in his or her assessment of an unknown person seeking advice. In addition, those aspects of life which make us happy are by no means always obvious. A common example is the retired couple who uproot themselves from the area they have lived in for many years in order to move to a seaside town because they have spent happy holidays there. The end result is frequently misery, because the couple does not realize the extent to which their previous happiness depended on the community of friends and neighbours they were used to.

Another reason why people often find it difficult to make themselves happy is because it would appear that happiness cannot be aimed for directly. You can successfully command yourself, "Be busy!", but ordering yourself, "Be happy!" is likely to prove no more successful than telling yourself, "Be spontaneous!". Happiness is frequently achieved as a by-product of pleasant and interesting events and activities, and too much questioning of one's emotional state can make it very hard to be happy. As has often been said, "You're not really happy if you have to think about it." Despite the apparent reasonableness of these arguments, we will see later in the chapter that it is actually possible to influence one's level of happiness by thinking about it and trying in a rather direct way to increase it.

Before we embark on a discussion of the various ways of increasing happiness, it is of interest to consider whether the pursuit of happiness deserves to be one of the primary goals of life. Some of the potential problems with turning life into a single-minded pursuit of happiness were vividly illustrated by Mark Twain in his story called *The Mysterious Stranger*. In this story, an angel promises an old man that he will make him happy. Unfortunately for the old man, the way in which the angel fulfils his promise is by making him insane. As a consequence, the old man is forced to spend the rest of his life in a mental institution, talking with imagined old friends and dispensing non-existent largesse.

The implications of this story are reasonably straightforward. Firstly, a happy life can still be a meaningless one. Secondly, having a useful and meaningful existence may very well ultimately prove to be more rewarding than simply being happy.

Mark Twain may seem to have demolished the notion that happiness should be the main goal of life, but such a conclusion may not be warranted. It was suggested at the beginning of this book that the happy person is someone who experiences much positive affect, relatively little negative affect, and whose thought processes reveal contentment at the general course of his or her life. Since the old man in the story presumably failed to fulfil the last of these requirements for happiness, he was not really happy in the full sense. Thus, Mark Twain has not succeeded in undermining the common desire for happiness, but has instead made us think more deeply about what it means to be happy.

In view of the complexities associated with happiness, it should come as no surprise to discover that several different approaches have been used to make people happier. We can draw a basic distinction between those approaches which focus on changing the unhappy person's environment and those which concentrate on changing the ways in which the environment is interpreted ("Do not do what you want, want what you do"). Happiness depends on the events which happen to an individual and on his or her interpretation of those events, and so both approaches to increasing happiness are potentially of great value.

The methods which have been used to make people happier can be distinguished from each other in another way. Some methods are designed primarily to reduce negative affect, whereas others attempt to increase positive affect. Most of the well-known approaches such as psychoanalysis concentrate far more on reducing negative affect than on promoting positive affect. This is not altogether surprising, since these approaches have been used to treat unhappy people with mood disorders such as anxiety and depression. Since psychoanalysis was the first systematic attempt by psychologists to increase human happiness, and since it remains very popular to this day, we will make a start by considering its usefulness. As we do so, it will be of interest to bear in mind the Marxist view that psychoanalysis and other forms of psychotherapy are merely "band aid" used to cover up genuine social problems. It is true, of course, that society is imperfect and that many anxious and depressed people have plenty to be anxious and depressed about. However, if we assume that society will always be a long way short of perfection, then it seems valuable to do whatever is possible to allow people to feel well-adjusted and comfortable within society.

PSYCHOANALYSIS

Sigmund Freud, the bearded Wunderkind from Vienna, was the first person to devise systematic techniques for alleviating unhappiness. He was struck (as have been many before and since) by the so-called "neurotic paradox", which is that neurotic individuals persistently behave in bizarre ways which breed unhappiness, and seem unable to benefit from experience. Freud made the startling assumption that most people have practically no clue as to the real nature of the forces motivating them. The neurotic individual is the helpless victim of concealed forces within the unconscious mind over which he or she has practically no control. The memories of nasty and traumatic events which may have occurred in early childhood lurk in the unconscious mind, and they cause the neurotic person to behave in a variety of abnormal ways.

The general outrage with which Freud's views were received was due mainly to his disgusting suggestion that the neurotic, middle-class ladies of Viennese society were almost literally bursting with repressed sexuality. However, some of the outrage was directed at the notion that the conscious mind is much less important than had been thought previously. According to Sigmund Freud, the unconscious mind is where the action is, with the thoughts of the conscious mind merely providing confusing and distorting reflections of the turbulence below.

Freud argued that the best way of reducing the unhappiness of his neurotic patients was by providing them with insight into the contents of their unconscious minds. Hypnosis, dream analysis, and word association were all brought into play in order to achieve this insight. When insight has been achieved, it can be used as a weapon to overwhelm the destructive conflicts housed within the unconscious mind. The bad news for us (but not necessarily for practising psychoanalysts) is that the business of gaining insight into one's unconscious mind is complex and extremely time-consuming, and can be achieved only with the expensive assistance of a qualified therapist.

According to Sigmund Freud, there is relatively little we can do by ourselves to cure neurotic unhappiness, because our conscious minds do not have access to most of the relevant information about the causes of our unhappiness. This limitation of the psychoanalytic approach would be tolerable if trained psychoanalysts were able to produce the goods by removing neuroses and increasing their patients' level of happiness. Many years ago my father examined the available evidence. He discovered that people undergoing psychoanalysis were somewhat less likely to recover than those receiving no treatment at all! Not surprisingly, this conclusion failed to find much favour among practitioners of psychoanalysis, and a rather bitter and heated controversy ensued.

Nowadays it is generally accepted that psychoanalysis is modestly effective in treating neurotic people and making their lives happier, but it is considerably less effective than its advocates have argued. In spite of the limited success of psychoanalysis, there is no doubt that, as Freud claimed, our unconscious minds often contain important information about the reasons for our unhappiness. However, it has proved very difficult to develop effective techniques for unravelling the mysteries of the unconscious, and there has been a big movement in recent years away from psychoanalysis and towards cognitive therapy.

COGNITIVE THERAPY

The so-called "cognitive revolution" in psychological treatment of unhappy people was spearheaded by American therapists Aaron Beck and Albert Ellis. In direct contrast to the psychoanalytic position, cognitive therapists put forward the encouraging claim that each individual has the key to understanding and resolving his or her psychological problems by focussing on conscious thoughts and feelings. This is very close to the common-sense view that, "We are what we think." The best known example of a cognitive approach to happiness is the advice given by Dale Carnegie, the author of *How to Win Friends and Influence People*. He suggested that as soon as you get up in the morning you should say to yourself, "Every day in every way I'm getting better and better!"

There seems to be some mileage in the Carnegie approach to mood enhancement. When people are given positive and upbeat statements to read and to think about, their mood does improve afterwards. However, the beneficial effects typically last for only about 15 or 20 minutes, so regular "topping up" would be needed to keep someone in a good mood.

Thinking positive thoughts is part of what is involved in cognitive therapy, but it is not the most crucial ingredient. The fundamental assumption made by cognitive therapists can be traced back nearly 2000 years to the Greek philosopher Epictetus. According to him, "It's not things or events that upset people but their view of these things." The important role of interpretation can be seen most clearly with respect to ambiguous events. A strange sound in the middle of the night can be interpreted as indicating that a burglar or rapist is in the house, and this interpretation will cause anxiety and unhappiness. Alternatively, it can be interpreted as being caused by a stray dog or cat, in which case no negative emotion is experienced.

In order to provide the reader with the information needed to become happier, it is important to consider cognitive therapy in some detail. We will start with the rational-emotive therapy proposed by Albert Ellis, and then move on to the somewhat different approach favoured by Aaron Beck.

Albert Ellis

Rational-emotive therapy can be summed up in the following forthright quotation from Albert Ellis: "The client is calmly, logically, forcefully taught that he'd better stop telling himself nonsense, accept reality, desist from condemning himself and others, and actively persist at making himself as happy as he can be in a world that is far from ideal." The starting point when attempting to make yourself happy, according to Ellis, is the realization that unhappiness occurs as the end point in a three-point sequence. Point A is the activating event, which might, for example, involve being rejected by someone else. Point B involves the individual's mixture of rational and irrational reactions to that event (e.g., "I can't stand being rejected! It is awful, horrible, and catastrophic for me not to be accepted!"). Finally point C is a state of great depression or unhappiness.

If you ask a person who has recently been rejected by someone they value to explain to you exactly why they are upset or depressed, he or she will nearly always reply that his or her emotional state stems from the fact of being rejected. Dr. Ellis robustly claims that this explanation is nonsensical. According to him, the real reason for the miserable emotional state is to be found in the exaggerated and melodramatic reactions to rejection which occur at point B in the sequence rather than the rejection itself.

The major way of restoring happiness proposed by Ellis's rational-emotive therapy is by altering those self-defeating thoughts which so frequently occur as a consequence of experiencing unpleasant life events. The essence of such therapy was expressed in the following pithy way by Dr. Ellis: "If he (i. e., the individual) wants to be minimally disturbable and maximally sane, he'd better substitute for all his absolutistic 'It's terrible's' two other words which he does not parrot or give lip-service to but which he incisively thinks through and accepts—namely, 'Too bad!' or 'Tough shit!'."

A concrete example of rational-emotive therapy in action involves a 25-year-old woman (whom we will call Cathy) who had never achieved an orgasm with her husband. Cathy was so concerned about this that she was ready to divorce her husband because of the shame she felt about their sexual ineptness. The approach used by Albert Ellis to persuade this young woman to think more rationally involved talking to her like this: "It seems clear that you are almost constantly telling yourself: 'Oh, how horrible I am because I never get an orgasm during intercourse!' and 'How can an incompetent person like me ever get a full climax?' ... But how can you possibly focus on your sex pleasure when you are agitatedly focusing on this kind of self-blaming? In order to feel sexually aroused, you must think of sexually-arousing things. And you are thinking of the most unarousing thing imaginable—that is, of your unworthiness as a woman."

In general terms, Ellis worked on persuading Cathy that her unsatisfactory sex life did not mean that she was worthless as a human being. As a result of therapy, she began to think along more rational lines. As time went by, she began to let herself go while engaged in sexual activity. Cathy even got to the point at which she decided to experiment with oral sex. She found this very arousing and exciting, but the state of high emotion made it difficult for her to focus properly on her own climax. This was sorted out when mutual oral-genital relations (sometimes called '69') were replaced by the husband performing cunnilingus, which gave her the perfect opportunity to concentrate solely on her own pleasure.

Cathy summed up her experience of cunnilingus in the following words: "Before I knew it, after only about five minutes of active intercourse, there it was, and it was thrilling as all hell. Other times, we had tried for a half hour or more and nothing had happened. But this time, wow!" Eventually, at the last therapy session, she told Albert Ellis about having spent most of the night having sex after her husband returned from a business trip: "And would you believe it, I'm sure that I had about a hundred orgasms during the night!"

What we have here (and in most other cases) is a genuine problem which is blown up out of all proportion. Cathy was right to be concerned about her unsatisfactory sex life. However, it was not rational to think that this problem meant that her marriage was of no value and should come to an end. It was also not rational for Cathy to regard her sexual difficulties as indicative of her general worthlessness. Many people have a tendency to turn minor problems into major ones in a similar way to Cathy, largely because of their adherence to irrational beliefs.

A useful starting point for changing any irrational beliefs you may have would be to write down what you think or feel about the various major unpleasant experiences you have had over the past year or so. Then scan through the list, and ask yourself which of your thoughts are excessive, over-the-top reactions to the events which caused them. These excessive reactions are the ones which need to be altered if you are to become happier.

Why do so many people have irrational beliefs which are so obviously fatal to their hopes of leading happy and contented lives? One of the main reasons is the nature of Western society. We are constantly bombarded with images and information encouraging us to aspire to an affluent and achievement-filled life. Television presents us with a succession of attractive, well-dressed, articulate, and successful people—for example, there is very little chance of someone old, ugly, and shabbily dressed reading the news. Advertising on television and elsewhere leads us to think that the possession of a bewildering variety of objects is necessary for the "good life" and the avoidance of failure. Schools, parents, and other influences can obviously be of enormous influence in persuading young people that success in the social, job, and financial domains is highly desirable. As a consequence, Albert Ellis has argued, millions of people subscribe to beliefs such as, "One should be competent and achieving in all areas", or "Anyone of value is able to make things turn out the way they want them to".

Aaron Beck

Aaron Beck agrees with Albert Ellis that distorted thoughts play a major role in producing and maintaining unhappy states. The nature of these thoughts differs somewhat in anxiety and in depression. Anxious people often have conditional or "if-then" thoughts (e.g., "If I fail the examination, then the future looks bleak"), whereas those who are depressed tend to have unconditional and absolute thoughts (e.g., "My limitations mean that I will always be a total failure"). The problem is that many of these thoughts are automatic in the sense that they keep recurring and often pass very rapidly through consciousness while the individual is involved in a social or work situation. Their short duration means that automatic thoughts can be very difficult to pay attention to and to remember subsequently.

The first stage in Beck's approach to cognitive therapy is to tell the patient about the existence of automatic thoughts, and to instruct him to go away and prepare as complete a list as possible of his automatic thoughts. The patient is told that the great majority of automatic thoughts deal with the way the person thinks about himself, his environment, or his future. The next step is for the therapist to write the patient's automatic thoughts on a blackboard. This has the advantage of literally distancing the patient from his thoughts. According to one patient, "I was able to get some perspective on my problems." Another patient declared, "I had to look at what I didn't want to face and this made it less scary."

What are the kinds of automatic thoughts reported by anxious and depressed patients? They naturally vary a lot from one person to another, but the following thoughts of patients with social problems are illustrative: "A situation or a person is unsafe until proven to be safe"; "Strangers despise weakness"; and "It is always best to assume the worst." Since patients rarely focus on these automatic thoughts, they have typically not addressed the issue of whether they should have such thoughts.

The patient and the therapist consider whatever automatic thoughts have been put on the blackboard, asking themselves how reasonable the thoughts would seem to normal people. In order to set the patient thinking more constructively, the therapist asks questions such as, "What is the evidence for or against this idea?" or "Are you thinking in all-or-none terms?" Unhappy people tend to think in ways which are grossly exaggerated, and their thoughts often contain extreme words such as "always", "never", and "must". The therapist tries to persuade the patient to tone down his thoughts so that, for example, "It is always difficult to get on with other people" becomes "It is sometimes easy to get on with other people, and sometimes not so easy."

Many patients are very restricted in their thinking. For example, a 24-year-old nurse who had recently been discharged from hospital after suffering from severe depression went to a party. A friend of hers called Jim asked her, "How are you feeling?" Her immediate reaction to this question was to think: "Jim thinks I am a basket case. I must really look bad for him to be concerned." Subsequently her therapist pointed out that she could equally well have interpreted Jim's question in completely different ways. His question might have indicated that he cared about her, or it might have been that he noticed that she looked better than she did before she went into hospital.

During the initial stages of therapy, the therapist focusses on persuading the patient to see how irrational many of his or her thoughts actually are. As treatment proceeds, the patient is encouraged to question his or her thoughts without the intervention of the therapist. Some of the questions which can usefully be asked about one's own thoughts are as follows: "What is the evidence for or against this idea?"; "Am I thinking in all-or-none terms?"; and "Am I using words or phrases which are extreme or exaggerated?"

Unhappy people are often irrational in their thinking because they attribute excessive blame to themselves if things go wrong. Indeed, they often feel that they are 100 per cent responsible for calamities which befall them. Cognitive therapy deals with this by asking the patient to focus on some future event which may have a negative outcome. The patient is then told to think of all of the factors which might influence the eventual outcome, to assess the relative importance of each factor, and to estimate the degree of personal control which he or she has over each factor. When this exercise has been completed, it is usually quite clear that it is absurd for the patient to accept total responsibility if the feared negative outcome materializes.

One of the difficulties which anxious patients have is their concern over the physical symptoms of anxiety. They frequently believe that other people always know when they are anxious, and devalue them as a consequence. The kind of thinking involved here is encapsulated in the old saying, "A thief always thinks his hat is on fire."

Aaron Beck has two main suggestions for those who find it hard to cope with the physical symptoms of anxiety. The first is to focus on the task in hand. The symptoms of anxiety are like a headache, in that both usually have much less effect if you refuse to attend to them. The second suggestion is to avoid saying to yourself, "Don't be anxious." This can produce exactly the opposite effect to that intended, just as saying to someone, "Don't spill the milk," may increase the chances that it will happen. It is much better to focus on the positive: say "Be alert" or "Carry the milk carefully."

CURING DEPRESSION: ACTIVITY

In their very different ways, Sigmund Freud and the cognitive therapists have argued that the best way of reducing unhappiness is by changing the unhappy person's perception of himself or herself and of the environment. This approach has had some success in curing patients suffering from depression, but it is not the whole story. For example, there is a common-sense view that people who are depressed should not sit around moping, but should actively involve themselves in something. Thus, 91 per cent of people agreed with the statement, "When feeling depressed, it usually helps to keep busy," and 65 per cent endorsed the statement, "When feeling depressed, it is most helpful to do something one enjoys." There is also a popular feeling that people who keep busy are less likely to become depressed in the first place.

Some American experts in clinical psychology argued that depressed patients should derive special benefit from engaging in more activities which they found pleasurable. To test this, the patients kept daily records of pleasant events and daily moods for a month. After that, computer analysis was used to work out which activities had the greatest enhancing effect on each person's mood. The patients were then encouraged to spend more time carrying out those activities. This pleasant-activities treatment was combined with training in social skills to make pleasant social events more available, and the treatment was successful in making the depressed patients considerably happier. A similar approach was taken with people who were not depressed who were asked to perform either two or twelve pleasurable activities which they had not engaged in for two weeks or more. Performing these pleasurable activities increased rated quality of life and feelings of pleasantness. This suggests that most people could make themselves happier by the simple expedient of devoting more time to pleasurable leisure-time activities.

Will spending more time in pleasurable pursuits always increase happiness? Not really, because pleasant activities have much less effect on mood if people are paid or pressured in some way to engage in those activities. With people who are severely depressed, there is the potential problem that they tend to interpret events in a rather negative fashion, and so they often fail to feel happy even when engaged in normally pleasant events. In spite of these limitations, the pleasant-activities approach is one of the simplest and most effect ways of reducing depression and increasing happiness.

CURING DEPRESSION AND ANXIETY: GOAL SETTING

How happy you are is much affected by the goals you have and by the success or otherwise of your efforts to attain those goals. In addition, there is some truth in the old adage, "It is better to travel hopefully than to arrive." In other words, there is much satisfaction and happiness to be obtained from simply moving towards life's goals.

There are two major ways in which goal setting can lead to a sense of unfulfilment and unhappiness. If someone sets himself a goal which is unrealistically difficult, then he is likely to experience anxiety when it becomes clear that the goal may not be achievable. There is overwhelming evidence that people whose aspirations are much higher than their achievements are dissatisfied and unhappy. On the other hand, if someone goes to the opposite extreme and refuses to pursue any goals at all, then the end result is likely to be depression. In order to avoid the unhappiness associated with anxiety or depression, it is important to pursue goals which are not too difficult. That was exactly what was found by Canadian psychologists Ted Palys and Brian Little, who also discovered that short-term goals are more associated with happiness than are long-term goals.

Depressed people are reluctant to formulate and pursue any meaningful goals, because they tend to be very pessimistic about their ability to attain such goals. This reluctance to set goals is a major reason why depressed individuals tend to be inactive, and we have already seen that their lack of activity helps to maintain the depressed state. This analysis suggests that depressed people might benefit from an approach in which they selected minor, realistic goals, and then rewarded themselves when these goals were achieved. This approach has been tried with depressed patients, and turned out to be more successful than various other forms of therapy. The combination of modest goal-setting and self-reward for achieving goals has also proved successful in increasing happiness among normal individuals who are not depressed. The main reason why this approach works so well is that it increases an individual's feelings of self-esteem. The belief that one has the ability and determination to cope with the demands of life is one of the cornerstones of both self-esteem and lasting happiness.

A PROGRAM FOR HAPPINESS

Numerous psychologists have provided readily accessible programs designed to increase human happiness. However, most of these programs are extremely difficult to evaluate. One reason is that much of the advice offered is rather vague. For example, William Nickels, author of *Win the Happiness Game*, exhorted his readers as follows: "Commit yourself 100 per cent to get as much out of life as you can. That is 100 per cent, not 99 per cent." That may be good advice, but how on earth would one go about following it? Another reason is that there is no proper scientific evidence of the effectiveness of most happiness programs, so that it is often difficult to tell whether they are really of any benefit at all.

A program designed to increase personal happiness which avoids the disadvantages of most other such programs was proposed by the American psychologist Michael Fordyce. He argued that there is no single magic formula for making people happier, but rather that the best way of increasing an individual's happiness level was to use a combination of several different techniques. On the basis of a substantial amount of exploratory work, he eventually evolved what he called the Fourteen Fundamentals Program. Each of the fundamentals consists of a specific behavioural and attitudinal objective which has been found to be characteristic of people who are generally happy.

What are the ingredients included by Michael Fordyce in his happiness program? The simplest thing to do is to quote his own description of them: "The fourteen fundamentals are as follows: (a) keep busy and be more active; (b) spend more time socializing; (c) be productive at meaningful work; (d) get better organized and plan things out; (e) stop worrying; (f) lower your expectations and aspirations; (g) develop positive, optimistic thinking; (h) become present oriented; (i) work on a healthy personality; (j) develop an outgoing, social personality; (k) be yourself; (l) eliminate negative feelings and problems; (m) close relationships are the number one source of happiness; (n) put happiness as your most important priority."

Fordyce provided people with instruction in various specific techniques designed to facilitate achieving these fundamentals. For example, in order to become more active, it was suggested that additional enjoyable activities should be scheduled in the daily routine. In order to stop worrying, the instruction was to keep a daily record of worries that ocurred to them, to analyze the amount of time spent worrying, to determine how many worries actually came true, and finally to use thought-substitution to avoid having worrying thoughts.

How effective is the Fourteen Fundamentals Program in increasing happiness? The findings have been extremely encouraging. In one study, 89 per cent of the participants claimed that the Program had helped them to stop, cope with, or stave off, unhappy moods. Eighty-one per cent indicated that the Program had increased their level of happiness, with 36 per cent claiming either extreme increases in happiness or much greater happiness. These impressive results actually under-estimate the true effects of the Program, because many of those whose happiness did not increase failed to make use of the Program in the suggested way. All of the fourteen fundamentals are useful in increasing happiness. However, many of those who have gone through the Program report that the most useful fundamentals are to stop worrying, to be oneself, and to develop positive, optimistic thinking. Of course, there are individual differences in which fundamentals are most effective, and the rule of thumb is that fundamentals which are perceived as an individual's weak points are the ones most worth concentrating on.

An important issue is whether the Fourteen Fundamentals Program has long-term beneficial effects on happiness, or whether it merely increases happiness for a rather brief period of time. Michael Fordyce contacted people who had been given the Program between nine and eighteen months previously. He discovered that 72 per cent felt that their long-term happiness had been increased by the Program, with 49 per cent claiming that the Program had made them far happier or a good deal happier than they would otherwise have been.

One of the most interesting features of the Fourteen Fundamentals Program is the comprehensive disproof it provides for the popular view that "pursuing happiness is the surest way to lose it." The entire Program focusses on happiness in a rather direct way and does not deal explicitly with the various problems and satisfactions of everyday life having an indirect effect on happiness. In addition, the reports of participants in the Fundamentals Program provide revealing evidence of its effectiveness. While they had always regarded happiness as a worthwhile goal, they had not previously set out in a deliberate fashion to increase their level of happiness. It was precisely the fact that the Program developed heightened awareness and understanding of happiness itself which they felt was instrumental in producing the increased levels of happiness which they experienced. As Michael Fordyce concluded, "Knowledge in any field can be enlightening and useful, and it appears that knowledge about human happiness is no different. Those who understand happiness have the best chance of attaining it."

One of the major reasons why the Fourteen Fundamentals Program is so successful is that it is a broadly-based approach. The fundamentals are designed to produce changes in three major areas: life style; attitudes and values; and personality. Maximal increase in happiness occurs when there are beneficial changes in all of these areas. It is thus simply not true that there is a single "golden rule" which can be used to produce increased happiness.

I have already mentioned the discovery by Michael Fordyce that the greatest increases in happiness tend to occur when people focus on those fundamentals where they are currently the weakest. Why should this be so? What is involved is the principle of diminishing returns. For example, if someone who is earning £100 a week receives a pay rise of £20 a week, he or she will certainly feel better off, whereas the same pay rise has practically no effect on the person earning £1000 a week. In similar fashion, following the fundamental of spending more time socializing by increasing one's socializing time by two hours a week is likely to have an important impact on someone who has previously spent no time at all socializing, but is unlikely to have a discernible effect on someone who has been in the habit of socializing every day in any case.

MEASURING HAPPINESS

The first step that is needed to make yourself happier is to have as great an understanding as possible of your current level of happiness. Accordingly, I have devised a special questionnaire for this book which allows you to assess your own happiness, and to compare it against the happiness of other people. This questionnaire is based on the fourteen fundamentals identified by Michael Fordyce, and it has the advantage that it will enable you to identify those fundamentals where you are currently the weakest. The scoring and interpretation of the scores are described after the questionnaire itself has been presented.

Happiness Questionnaire

Consider each statement in turn, and decide how true it is for you personally. If it is completely true for you, circle the "9" to the right of the statement. If it is completely untrue for you, circle the "1" to the right of the statement. If the truth of the statement lies somewhere between these two extremes, circle a number between "2" and "8" indicating the extent to which it is true, with "5" indicating that the statement is neither true nor untrue.

1.	I am busier than other people.	1 2 3 4 5 6 7 8 9
2.	I have numerous leisure activities to occupy me.	1 2 3 4 5 6 7 8 9
3.	I am nearly always "on the go."	1 2 3 4 5 6 7 8 9
4.	I definitely have more friends than most people.	1 2 3 4 5 6 7 8 9
5.	I socialize several times in the average week.	1 2 3 4 5 6 7 8 9
6.	I really love spending time with other people.	1 2 3 4 5 6 7 8 9
7.	I find my work extremely interesting.	1 2 3 4 5 6 7 8 9
8.	Time usually flies when I am working.	1 2 3 4 5 6 7 8 9
9.	I usually work very efficiently.	1 2 3 4 5 6 7 8 9
10.	My life is carefully organized.	1 2 3 4 5 6 7 8 9

11. I can nearly always lay my hands on important documents
    almost immediately.   1 2 3 4 5 6 7 8 9
12. I usually have enough time each week to do what I want
    to do.   1 2 3 4 5 6 7 8 9
13. I worry more than most people.   1 2 3 4 5 6 7 8 9
14. I usually find it impossible to keep worrying thoughts out
    of my mind.   1 2 3 4 5 6 7 8 9
15. Life is a very worrying business.   1 2 3 4 5 6 7 8 9
16. I take life very much as it comes.   1 2 3 4 5 6 7 8 9
17. I do not have any great unfulfilled aspirations.   1 2 3 4 5 6 7 8 9
18. I expect the future to be very much like the past.   1 2 3 4 5 6 7 8 9
19. I am generally very optimistic about things.   1 2 3 4 5 6 7 8 9
20. I am confident that my life will turn out well.   1 2 3 4 5 6 7 8 9
21. I generally anticipate that things will work out for the best. 1 2 3 4 5 6 7 8 9
22. I think about the present much more than about the past
    or the future.   1 2 3 4 5 6 7 8 9
23. The "here and now" is of absorbing interest.   1 2 3 4 5 6 7 8 9
24. I always try to live "for the moment."   1 2 3 4 5 6 7 8 9
25. My friends regard me as very well-adjusted.   1 2 3 4 5 6 7 8 9
26. I am nearly always cheerful.   1 2 3 4 5 6 7 8 9
27. I generally "bounce back" from adversity.   1 2 3 4 5 6 7 8 9
28. I am more outgoing than most people.   1 2 3 4 5 6 7 8 9
29. People think of me as being very sociable.   1 2 3 4 5 6 7 8 9
30. I am a particularly friendly person.   1 2 3 4 5 6 7 8 9
31. I never "put on an act" with other people.   1 2 3 4 5 6 7 8 9
32. I am content just to be myself.   1 2 3 4 5 6 7 8 9
33. I have no wish to be like anyone else.   1 2 3 4 5 6 7 8 9
34. I do not feel that my problems are insuperable.   1 2 3 4 5 6 7 8 9
35. I don't waste any of my time envying other people.   1 2 3 4 5 6 7 8 9
36. I very rarely experience frustration and anger.   1 2 3 4 5 6 7 8 9
37. I have a very close relationship with a member of the
    opposite sex.   1 2 3 4 5 6 7 8 9
38. My family life has always been very loving.   1 2 3 4 5 6 7 8 9
39. I have more exceptionally close friends than most other
    people.   1 2 3 4 5 6 7 8 9
40. I always do what I can to be happy.   1 2 3 4 5 6 7 8 9
41. I regard being happy as the main goal in life.   1 2 3 4 5 6 7 8 9
42. I would rather be a happy pig than an unhappy Socrates.   1 2 3 4 5 6 7 8 9
43. I am much happier than most people.   1 2 3 4 5 6 7 8 9
44. I am somewhat unhappy much of the time.   1 2 3 4 5 6 7 8 9
45. I wish I could be happier.   1 2 3 4 5 6 7 8 9

Scoring

The items in the questionnaire are scored in groups of three. In order to score your answers, work out your total score for the first three items (1-3), the second three items (4-6), and so on. Matters are a little more complicated for the final set of three items (43-45). For item 43, subtract the number you circled from 10 (e.g., if you circled the 6, then record $10 - 6 = 4$). Add this to the numbers circled on items 44 and 45 to give the total for this final set.

Items 1–3 deal with the fundamental of keeping busy and active. The average score is 16.5, and your score is rather low if it is 13 or less.

Items 4–6 deal with the fundamental of spending much time socializing. The average score is 17.6, and your score is rather low if it is 13 or less.

Items 7–9 deal with the fundamental of being productive at meaningful work. The average score is 20.9, and your score is rather low if it is 17 or less.

Items 10–12 deal with the fundamental of being well organized and planning things out. The average score is 16.8, and your score is rather low if it is 14 or less.

Items 13–15 deal with the fundamental of stopping worrying. The average score is 12.6, but note that here a low score is indicative of happiness. A score of 16 or more is rather high.

Items 16–18 deal with the fundamental of lowering your expectations and aspirations. The average score is 11.7, and a score of 7 or below is rather low.

Items 19–21 deal with the fundamental of developing positive and optimistic thinking. The average score is 19.8, and your score is rather low if it is 16 or less.

Items 22–24 deal with the fundamental of becoming present-oriented. The average score is 14.1, and a score of 10 or less is rather low.

Items 25–27 deal with the fundamental of working on a healthy personality. The average score is 19.7, and a score of 16 or less is rather low.

Items 28–30 deal with the fundamental of developing an outgoing, social personality. The average score is 16.6, and a score of 12 or less is rather low.

Items 31–33 deal with the fundamental of being yourself. The average score is 20.5, and a score of 12 is rather low.

Items 34–36 deal with the fundamental of eliminating negative feelings and problems. The average score is 18.0, and a score of 14 or less is rather low.

Items 37–39 deal with the fundamental of close relationships. The average score is 19.1, and a score of 15 or less is rather low.

Items 40–42 deal with the fundamental of putting happiness as your most important priority. The average score is 19.6, and a score of 15 or below is rather low.

Items 43–45 deal with your overall level of happiness. The average score (details of how to calculate it are given above) is 12.8, but note that a low score is indicative of happiness. A score of 15 or more is rather high.

Interpretation

The score on items 43–45 provides an indication of whether you are generally happier or less happy than other people. Even if your overall level of happiness is greater than that of most other people, it may still be the case that there are specific areas in which your level of happiness is relatively low. This is where the scores on the fourteen fundamentals come in. These fourteen scores enable you to see the pattern of your personal strong and weak points in   the happiness stakes, by comparing yourself against other people on each fundamental.

If you are really interested in becoming happier, then it is important to identify those fundamentals where your score is lower than that of most other people. Obviously, it does not really matter if your score on a fundamental is only just below the average score, but it may be a matter of concern if your score is substantially below the average. Accordingly, for each fundamental I have identified a score which is rather low in the sense that only one quarter of the population obtains a score as low as that. Concentrate your efforts to increase your level of happiness on those fundamentals where your score is rather low, and you may be pleasantly surprised at the beneficial effects that occur as a result.

CHAPTER EIGHT

Unhappiness Can Kill You

Some people have argued that it is somewhat frivolous to make the pursuit of happiness one of the major goals in life. According to them, there are far more important goals to strive for. For example, one should try to achieve a worthwhile and successful career, or to be of service to the community, or to develop spiritual values instead of being overly concerned about happiness. It has even been suggested by some tough-minded individuals that happiness can breed complacency, and that a healthy dose of unhappiness can drive people onwards to greater achievements.

In my opinion, these views are profoundly misguided. While hardly anyone would deny that it is important to do one's best to make a reasonable contribution to the well-being of society by one's efforts, there is absolutely no reason why this has to be at the expense of personal happiness. Indeed, as we saw in an earlier chapter, people who are unselfish tend to be much happier than those who are selfish, so that helping others actually enhances happiness.

An extremely important reason why people should concentrate on maximizing their own level of happiness is because there is a fairly strong association between happiness and health. There are, of course, various possible reasons why low levels of happiness and ill health should go together. The most obvious is because those who are unwell often live rather limited and painful lives, and these negative features of their lives cause them to feel unhappy. Of course, poor health can cause unhappiness. It is also possible that there is some other factor which influences both happiness and health. For example, those of low socio-economic status tend to be less happy than those of high socio-economic status, and they also suffer more from health problems. Thus, there may not be a direct link at all between health and happiness.

However, this chapter will focus on the interesting possibility that there is a direct link between happiness and health, with unhappiness causing poor health and even premature death. In other words, the length of your life may depend on your level of happiness. If that is true, then there could be few more powerful reasons for regarding happiness as one of the most important goals in life.

LIFE-STYLES

It is well-known that unhappiness in the form of stress can have negative effects on people's health. In particular those under stress are more likely than unstressed individuals to catch colds, flu, and all kinds of common diseases. The notion that unhappiness could have much more devastating effects on health was first convincingly shown in California during the 1970s by Berkman and Syme. A team of researchers made use of interviews to investigate 7000 people with different life-styles, focussing especially on the strength of their supportive social networks. At one extreme were those unfortunate individuals who lived alone and who had very limited good social support from family and from friends. At the other extreme were individuals who had strong social networks, including close family ties and several good friends. From all that we know about happiness, there is no doubt at all that those with the very supportive social networks were much happier than the social isolates.

Nine years after the initial assessment of the social satisfaction of these Californians, the researchers made enquiries in order to find out how many of them were still alive. The figures were very surprising. Consider, for example, men who were in their fifties at the time of the original interview. Of the happy middle-aged men who had the most social connections, only 10 per cent had died during the nine-year interval. This compares with a massive 31 per cent of the unhappy men with the fewest social connections! In other words, socially dissatisfied men were three times as likely to die as those who were socially satisifed.

The figures for women were very nearly as dramatic. Of those women in their sixties who were socially dissatisfied, 29% had died, compared with only 10 per cent of those who had strongly supportive social networks. These stunning figures suggested that the unhappiness of loneliness and relative social isolation could kill you. This may sound like a far-fetched idea. However, unhappy people are less likely than happy people to adopt good health practices (e.g., taking regular exercise) and eating and drinking in moderation, and this poor health-related behaviour could very plausibly affect their life expectancy.

This possibility was explored by the researchers in California. As expected, they obtained some support for the notion that the poor health practices of lonely and unhappy people contribute to the shortening of their lives. However, Berkman and Syme also discovered that those with strong social networks were more likely than those with weak networks to survive the nine-year period, even when the two groups were matched in terms of health practices, obesity, smoking, drinking, and initial health.

Recent findings in the United Kingdom have suggested that it is almost literally true that you can "die of a broken heart." Married men were compared with divorced or separated men of the same age. The divorced or separated men were more than twice as likely as the married men to die of heart disease, seven times as likely to die of cirrhosis of the liver, and ten times as likely to die of TB. Interestingly, women appear less likely than men to die of a broken heart. Divorced or separated women were only slightly more likely than married women to die of heart disease, four times as likely to die of cirrhosis, and two and a half times as likely to die of TB. Why do divorced and separated people die sooner than married ones? Probably the single most important reason is that they generally take less care of themselves. Divorced and separated people typically drink and smoke more than married people, and they also tend to take less physical exercise. All of these differences conspire to make them more vulnerable to many different diseases.

MY JOB IS KILLING ME!

The media in recent years have devoted more and more attention to so-called "executive stress" "executive burnout", and the like. There is no doubt at all that jobs which are complex and involve great time pressure create anxiety and tension, but do they have the damaging long-term consequences implied by a term such as "executive burnout"? Some light has been shed on this issue by looking at the relationship between job satisfaction (which is presumably low in those in very stressful jobs) and physical health. When a very wide range of jobs was considered, it was discovered that job satisfaction correlated approximately 0.26 with length of life. It thus appears that having a job which is low in satisfaction can have disastrous consequences in the long run.

We can compare different jobs in terms of what is known as the "mortality rate". A mortality rate of 100 per cent for a particular kind of job means that people doing that job are neither more nor less likely to die in any given year than are people in general. A mortality rate of 50 per cent means that those doing that job are only half as likely to die as people in general, and a mortality rate of 200 per cent means that they are twice as likely to die in any given year. In terms of this mortality rate, clergymen are the most favoured workers. Their mortality rate is a reassuring 76 per cent. At the other extreme, labourers have a mortality rate of 273 per cent, and sailors one of 233 per cent.

Some of the most striking findings concern the association between job satisfaction and death from heart disease, where correlations as large as -0.8 have been reported. It was found a few years ago that university lecturers were the most satisfied group (93 per cent satisfied) and their rate of heart attacks was only 71 per cent of the national average. As a Professor at the University of London, I have the distinct impression that one of the fruits of the Thatcher Revolution has been to produce a considerable reduction in job satisfaction in the academic community, and perhaps this will lead in a few years to an epidemic of heart attacks among academics! Managers were about average for job satisfaction, with 69 per cent being satisfied, and they have 16 per cent more heart attacks than the national average. The least satisfied group were unskilled car workers, of whom only 16 per cent expressed satisfaction with their jobs. They suffered for this dissatisfaction by having a rate of heart attacks which was 176 per cent of the national average.

HEALTHY AND UNHEALTHY
PERSONALITIES

We saw earlier in the book that personality plays a major role in determining happiness. In essence, non-neurotic extraverts are the happiest group of people and neurotic introverts are the unhappiest group. One might, therefore, predict that neurotic introverts should be especially susceptible to all sorts of physical diseases, whereas stable extraverts should be relatively invulnerable. Unfortunately, matters are not as simple as that. Nevertheless, the incidence of heart disease and cancer does vary considerably from one personality group to another, as we will see.

Individuals high in neuroticism are much less happy than those who are low in neuroticism, and they have been found to suffer from many more headaches and stomach aches. More importantly, those who are high in neuroticism or anxiety are more likely than other people to have heart attacks and to die from heart disease. It has also been found that sufferers from heart disease are on average high in hostile aggression, which is another ingredient of the unhappy personality.

Neuroticism and hostile aggression both form part of the so-called Type A personality. Those with Type A personality are competitive, aggressive, moody, with high job involvement, and are very strongly motivated to achieve success. Type A's have been discovered to be twice as likely as other people to have heart attacks, even after other factors such as cholesterol level, amount of smoking, and age are held constant.

Those who are most vulnerable to cancer have a rather different type of personality. In a large-scale study in Chicago, depression (which is an important aspect of unhappiness) was assessed in 2000 industrial workers. It was then seen which of them died of cancer during the following 17 years. The workers who died of cancer tended to be those who were very depressed at the time of original testing. Depression predicted death from cancer even when family history of cancer, smoking, drinking, and age were controlled statistically. Cancer is related to depressing events as well as to depressed personality. There is now rather strong evidence that the loss of significant people or objects (e.g., death of a loved one; loss of a valued job) can contribute to the development of cancer.

Cancer-prone individuals tend to be rather inhibited about the expression of their emotions. As a consequence, they come across as being very patient and passive. Not only does this over-controlled personality style cause vulnerability to cancer, but it also reduces the duration of life after cancer has been diagnosed. Those cancer sufferers who manage to survive the longest are those who actively attempt to fight the disease rather than passively accepting it.

It is all very well for researchers to show that aspects of the unhappy personality can cause both heart disease and cancer. However, what we would all like to know is whether any of this knowledge can be used in order to prevent people from developing these potentially fatal diseases in the first place. Exciting evidence that precisely this may be possible has been obtained very recently in West Germany. Cancer-prone and coronary-prone individuals were given a special type of therapy designed to change their emotions and behaviour away from those making them vulnerable to these diseases. Part of this therapy involved reducing their negative and unhappy emotional states. Equal numbers of cancer-prone and coronary-prone individuals were not given any therapy, so that the effectiveness of therapy could be assessed.

The results were remarkably encouraging. In a follow-up 13 years later, none of the 50 cancer-prone individuals who had received therapy had died from cancer. In contrast, cancer had killed 16 of the 50 cancer-prone individuals who had not received therapy. Among the coronary-prone individuals, only three out of the 46 receiving therapy had died of heart disease or a stroke during the 13-year interval, compared with 16 out of 46 not receiving therapy.

UNHAPPINESS THE KILLER

Individuals can be unhappy for many different reasons. Some are unhappy because they are socially isolated, whether due to divorce or to some other reason. Others are unhappy because their jobs are very stressful and demanding. Still others are unhappy because their personalities make them anxious, depressed, or hostile. Unhappiness produced in any of these ways makes an individual vulnerable to physical illness, and can prove fatal in the long run.

There are various reasons why unhappiness can be a killer. Unhappy emotional states which last for a long time can affect the physiological system in various damaging ways, and disturb the functioning of the immune system. Unhappiness can also make people less inclined to look after themselves properly. Excessive smoking and drinking, combined with insufficient physical exercise, can set the scene for future illness and premature death.

The good news is that it may be possible in the future to use therapy to improve matters. If therapy can be used to prevent cancer and heart disease, then presumably it could be used with success to reduce the incidence of other, less serious, health problems. It is too early to know the extent to which psychological treatment will be able to guard against ill health, but at least there is light at the end of the tunnel.

CHAPTER NINE

Destroying the Myths about Happiness

We have all had the experience of being happy and of being unhappy, and we have all observed happiness and unhappiness in other people. As a result, many people feel they are experts on the topic of happiness. This claimed expertise, however, is often illusory. There is a natural tendency for us to assume that what is true of our lives is generally true of other people's lives. Thus, if someone has discovered that he is happier in the married state than he was when he was single, he may conclude that marriage increases human happiness. On the other hand, someone whose level of happiness has gone down after marriage may well decide that marriage is an outmoded, happiness-demolishing institution.

The fallacy in attempting to draw general conclusions solely on the basis of one's own experience is obvious. However, there is also a less straightforward problem with trying to understand happiness from the perspective of one's own life. Someone who is less happy after marriage than before may well be inclined to attribute his decreased happiness to marriage, but this may not be correct. His life will undoubtedly have changed in various ways over the years: he has grown older, perhaps acquired fresh work responsibilities, suffered the loss of loved ones, and so on. It is, thus, very difficult for him to work out exactly which changes in his life have played a part in making him less happy than he was before his marriage. The only satisfactory way of identifying the factors which produce happiness and unhappiness is by collecting a substantial body of information from large samples of people. This allows us, for example, to compare married with unmarried people of the same age, while equating the two groups in terms of all of the other relevant factors. This approach is, of course, the one which has been followed by psychologists, and which has formed the basis for this entire book. We have encountered numerous cases in which common-sense views have been disproved by psychological research, and this chapter provides a summary of these discrepancies between popular opinions about happiness and the factual evidence.

THE MYTHS

Myth 1:   Your level of happiness depends simply on the number and nature of the pleasurable events which happen to you. Of course, it is indisputable that the number and nature of the pleasurable events you experience play a part in determining how happy you are. However, their importance is generally grossly exaggerated. Pleasurable events may enhance happiness at the time of their occurrence, but their effects on the level of happiness tend to be transient. Highly pleasurable events have the disadvantage that they can make subsequent moderately pleasurable ones seem uninteresting in comparison, and thus actually lower the level of happiness in the long run.

Much more important than pleasurable events in determining your level of happiness is your personality. Some people characteristically interpret life's events in a positive and optimistic way, whereas other people are chronically negative and pessimistic in their reactions to events. As the American psychologist Ed Diener put it, "A person enjoys pleasures because he or she is happy, not vice versa."

Myth 2:   The rapid changes and stresses in modern Western society have made people less happy than they were in the simpler times of yesteryear. When Americans were asked whether people were happier during the old horse-and-buggy days than they are today, approximately two-thirds of them agreed that they were. There are certainly biological reasons for arguing that we are designed for an active, out-of-doors existence which is quite different from the sedentary, desk-bound jobs which tens of millions endure in contemporary Western society. It could also be argued that the increased pace of life nowadays makes us highly stressed and so unhappier than our forefathers with their more relaxed life-styles.

There is some truth in the above arguments, but they do not tell the whole story. Films dealing with past eras tend to paint far too rosy a picture, emphasizing the attractive features and ignoring negative aspects such as grinding poverty, poor physical health, and the lack of variety in most people's lives. When all of these factors are taken into account, it begins to make sense that people are on average significantly happier than they were many years ago. The notion that modern Western society does not prevent people from being happy is also supported by the finding that people in developed countries are generally happier than those in under-developed countries.

Myth 3:   If you have some serious physical disability, you will be much less happy than other people. A serious physical disability such as paralysis or blindness greatly limits the ability to engage in numerous everyday activities. Of course, there are wheelchairs for paralyzed people and guide dogs and Braille books for the blind, but it cannot be claimed that these forms of assistance permit disabled people to function normally. As a consequence, it is natural to assume that those with severe physical disabilities should become bitter and unhappy when they compare themselves to other, physically healthy, people.

There is a small element of truth in Myth 3, in that those who become physically disabled are usually rather unhappy for several months afterwards. However, what is more striking is that their level of happiness eventually recovers to approximately the normal level. The reason for this is that happiness depends on the discrepancy between what happens to you and what you expect to happen. There is a necessary period of adjustment after becoming physically disabled during which expectations gradually change; after that, physically disabled people are very nearly as happy as those who are physically healthy.

Myth 4:   Young people in the prime of life are generally much happier than older people. Middle-aged people often look enviously at the life-styles of young people in their late teens and early twenties. By and large, young people have relatively few responsibilities, their lives have expanding horizons, and they have the freedom and the opportunity to experiment romantically and sexually. In contrast, middle-aged people often feel that their own lives follow a rather set pattern and that the future is unlikely to offer many exciting developments. The apparent advantages enjoyed by young people have led many people to conclude that young people are usually a lot happier than older people.

In fact, there is no good evidence that young people are particularly happy. When happiness is looked at in more detail, it is usually found that contentment and satisfaction both rise with age. Young people are characterized by stronger levels of both positive and negative affect than older people, and are thus more emotional. However, since happiness consists of high positive affect and low negative affect, the average level of happiness is relatively little affected by age.

Myth 5:   People who experience a lot of happiness also experience a lot of unhappiness. It is often suggested that people can be divided into those who are rather emotional and those who are unemotional. Those who are emotional experience the highs and the lows of emotional experience, whereas those who are unemotional experience neither great happiness nor great unhappiness. In other words, in order to have the capacity to feel euphoric you must also have the capacity to feel utterly wretched and in the depths of despair.

It is true that some individuals (mostly neurotic extraverts) experience much happiness and unhappiness in their lives, whereas others (stable introverts) remain unemotional and relatively unaffected by most of life's events. However, there are other groups of individuals who serve to disprove Myth 5. The luckiest people are the stable extraverts: they tend to experience a lot of happiness, but the fact that they are stable rather than neurotic means that they are unhappy only relatively infrequently. Those individuals who have drawn the short straw in life are the neurotic introverts. They are rather anxious and so spend much of their time feeling thoroughly miserable and unhappy. However, they do not have the compensation of experiencing great happiness.

Thus, some of the people who experience a lot of happiness also experience a lot of unhappiness, but others do not. Similarly, some of those who are frequently unhappy also experience much happiness, but others do not. In other words, Myth 5 is a myth because it is a gross over-simplification of a complex reality.

Myth 6:   More intelligent individuals are generally happier than less intelligent ones. Intelligence is a highly prized resource in Western society. Those who are highly intelligent tend to be members of the higher social classes, they usually have well-paid and interesting jobs, and their children tend to be intelligent and successful academically. In contrast, the relatively unintelligent are found mostly in the lower social classes, they have poorly paid and boring jobs, and their children tend to be unintelligent.

Expressed in those terms, it seems highly probable that there would be a positive relationship between intelligence and happiness. In fact, the usual finding is that intelligence is completely unrelated to the level of happiness. How can this be in view of the very tangible benefits associated with high intelligence? What is generally forgotten is that highly intelligent individuals tend to have much higher aspirations than those who are less intelligent. Since happiness is associated with having aspirations which are in line with achievement, the high aspirations of the intelligent can prevent them from being happy.

There may also be some truth in the old saying, "Only cows are contented." In other words, to be happy you need to be oblivious to the various problems of life and of society. Intelligent people are more aware of the dangers of nuclear power, the nuclear arms race, and so on, and their knowledge of such matters may reduce the level of happiness.

Myth 7:   Children usually add significantly to the happiness of a married couple. It is often assumed that children are the "icing on the cake" so far as married couples are concerned. In many people's eyes, having children is the most important reason for getting married, and most married couples look forward with eager anticipation to the patter of little feet. The fact that most couples do not stop with one child but continue to have one or more additional children seems to confirm the notion that children are a source of great happiness. Surprising though it may seem, there is overwhelming evidence that children significantly reduce marital happiness. This reduction in happiness is especially great for married women, but is also found in married men. We can be certain that it is the presence of children which causes the reduced happiness, because most married couples become happier again as soon as all of their children have left the family nest.

Myth 8:   Winning a fortune would make anyone feel happier. When Americans were asked whether becoming 25 per cent better off financially would make them happier, an overwhelming percentage claimed that it would. They were not asked the further question whether they felt that winning a fortune on the football pools or on a lottery would make them happier, but it is probably safe to assume that an even higher percentage would have argued that it would do so. The ability to buy almost anything one wants without needing to worry about the financial implications is so obviously desirable that it is not surprising that people answered as they did.

Despite the obvious advantages of suddenly winning a huge amount of money, there is no evidence to suggest that the winners are much happier than other people. Indeed, what is really striking about most of the winners is how little their spending patterns are affected by the win. The typical pattern is to buy a better house and car, and then to invest most of the rest of the money for the future. On the negative side, winning a fortune often has various disruptive effects. These include being treated differently by other people, giving up work, losing one's social identity, and sometimes seeing one's marriage collapse. In view of the disruption, it makes sense that those who do win a fortune are typically hardly any happier than they were before their big win.

Myth 9:   Men are happier than women. It is often argued that women are more sensitive than men, and as a result they are more bruised and upset when misfortunes occur. This sensitivity prevents women from being entirely happy. In contrast, it has been claimed that men are less affected by adversity, and so are less inclined to tears and other manifestations of unhappiness. This line of argument leads to the conclusion that men are typically rather happier than women.

There is a grain of truth in the above line of reasoning, but the wrong conclusion is drawn. It is true that women are more sensitive emotionally than men ("With women the heart argues, not the mind": Matthew Arnold), but they are more responsive to pleasant events as well as to unpleasant events. As a consequence, women experience more positive affect and more negative affect than men. In terms of the overall level of happiness, there is practically no difference between men and women. However, young women are slightly happier than young men, and the opposite is true from middle age onwards.

Myth 10:   Pursuing happiness directly is the surest way to lose it. It is often argued that happiness occurs as a by-product of other activities, and that it does not make any sense to aim for it directly. In other words, happiness occurs in a natural way, and it cannot be produced to order by thinking about it. This viewpoint is summed up in the old adage, "You're not really happy if you have to think about it."

Despite the popularity of this view of happiness, it appears to be profoundly mistaken. The opposite position is that anything can be done more effectively when we possess the relevant knowledge. This is accepted by everyone when it comes to building a bridge or writing a book, but is often rejected so far as something as apparently fragile as the emotional state of happiness is concerned. Michael Fordyce has devised a Fourteen Fundamentals Program which requires the participants to pursue happiness in a very direct way. Rather than destroying people's happiness, this direct assault on happiness has proved remarkably effective in increasing happiness. The success of this program disproves the notion that pursuing happiness is the surest way to lose it.

Myth 11:   Happiness is a rather superficial goal to pursue. Many people have claimed that happiness is a relatively frivolous goal, being related to such superficialities as the advertisers' vision of "the good life". Instead, it is much better to strive for solid achievements at work, in the community, and in one's inner or spiritual well-being. Those of an authoritarian bent have even argued that unhappiness may serve a useful function, spurring people on to work harder and to improve themselves.

The notion that happiness is not a significant matter is misguided. Firstly, it does not make much sense to draw a distinction between happiness on the one hand and solid achievements on the other, because solid achievements increase both self-esteem and happiness. Secondly, happiness is linked with physical health and is even predictive of longevity. Since unhappiness can kill you, it cannot be said that happiness is of little or no consequence. Thirdly, happy people work better, have more social contacts, enjoy sex more, and have more leisure activities than those who are unhappy. It would be ludicrous to suggest that all of these effects of being happy are inconsequential.

Myth 12:   Happiness is a fleeting experience. According to the 18th-century poet Thomas Gray, " . . . sorrow comes too late, and happiness too swiftly flies." Many have agreed with Gray that happiness is a fleeting experience, and have bemoaned the way in which it fails to last for long after some pleasurable event has come to an end.

It is true that joy tends to be short-lived, but the same is not generally true of happiness. When people are asked how happy they are on two occasions separated by a period of two or three years, they tend to give similar answers each time. Happiness is fairly stable over time because it is based upon the amount of satisfaction with the way in which one's life is progressing. The stability of happiness is also due to the fact that an individual's level of happiness is affected very much by his or her personality, and personality changes relatively little over time.

Myth 13:   Marriage is an outmoded institution which tends to reduce happiness. The fact that one marriage in three now ends in divorce lends force to the notion that marriage is an institution which has outlived itse usefulness. Those who feel that marriage is conducive to unhappiness can also point to the loss of freedom and the substantial demands which marriage imposes upon married couples. The loss of freedom, it has been proposed, is more irksome to men than to women, since men are naturally promiscuous.

Those who feel that marriage still has a future note that most divorced people seem remarkably willing to re-marry. If marriage is so terrible, why are so many divorced people prepared to sample it for a second time? The evidence indicates strongly that marriage is good for you. Married people are much happier than those who are not married. The idea that men gain less than women from marriage is quite wrong: if anything, men gain more from marriage than women in terms of satisfaction and happiness. More detailed analysis of happiness in the married and the not married reveals that married people have higher levels of positive affect and lower levels of negative affect than those who are not married. Thus, despite the complexities of contemporary marriage, it is usually better to be married rather than single.

CONCLUSIONS

It would be ludicrous to pretend that psychologists have discovered everything there is to be known about happiness. However, as this chapter has demonstrated, our knowledge of happiness has moved well beyond the limited insights of common sense. Most of this advance in knowledge has occurred over the past 20 years or so. At this rate, we may know so much about happiness by the beginning of the 21st century that the world will be full of happy people.

Further Reading

Chapter 1

James, W. (1960). *The Varieties of Religious Experience*. London: Fontana.

Maslow, A.H. (1959). Cognition of being in the peak experiences. *Journal of Genetic Psychology*, *94*, 43–66.

Chapter 2

Costa, P.T., & McCrae, R.R. (1980). Influence of extraversion and neuroticism on subjective well-being: Happy and unhappy people. *Journal of Personality and Social Psychology*, *38*, 668–678.

Lynn, R. (1971). *Personality and National Character*. Oxford: Pergamon.

Russell, J.A., & Mehrabian, A. (1977). Evidence for a three-factor theory of emotions. *Journal of Research in Personality*, *11*, 273–294.

Warr, P., Barter, J., & Brownbridge, G. (1983). On the independence of positive and negative affect. *Journal of Personality and Social Psychology*, *44*, 644–651.

Chapter 3

Eysenck, H.J. (1976). *Sex and Personality*. London: Open Books.

Eysenck, H.J., & Wilson, G.D. (1979). *The Psychology of Sex*. London: Dent.

Fisher, S. (1973). *The Female Orgasm*. New York: Basic Books.

Giese, H., & Schmidt, A. (1968). *Studenten Sexualitat*. Hamburg: Rowohlt.

Chapter 4

Adams, V. (1980). Getting at the heart of jealousy. *Psychology Today*, *13*, 38–47.

Branden, N. (1980). *The Psychology of Romantic Love*. Los Angeles: J.P. Tarcher.

Diener, M., & Pyszcynski, T.A. (1978). Effects of erotica upon men's loving and liking responses for women they love. *Journal of Personality and Social Psychology*, *36*, 1302–1309.

Lee, J.A. (1977). A typology of styles of loving. *Personality and Social Psychology Bulletin*, *3*, 173–182.

Rubin, Z. (1973). From liking to loving: Patterns of attraction in dating relationships. In T.L. Houston (Ed.), *Foundations of Interpersonal Attraction*. New York: Academic Press.

Sternberg, R.J., & Grajek, S. (1984). The nature of love. *Journal of Personality and Social Psychology*, *47*, 312–329.

Walster, E., & Walster, G.W. (1978). *A New Look at Love*. Reading, MA: Addison-Wesley.

Chapter 5

Andrews, F.M., & Withey, S.B. (1976). *Social Indicators of Well-Being: Americans' Perceptions of Life Quality*. New York: Plenum Press.

Bradburn, N. (1969). *The Structure of Psychological Well-Being*. Chicago: Aldine.

Campbell, A., Converse, P.E., & Rodgers, W.L. (1976). *The Quality of American Life: Perceptions, Evaluations, and Satisfactions*. New York: Russell Sage Foundation.

Cooper, C., & Payne, R.L. (Eds.) (1980). *Current Concerns in Occupational Stress*. Chichester: Wiley.

Rubenstein, C. (1980). *Psychology Today*. 13 May, 62–76.

Chapter 6

Brickman, P., & Campbell, D.T. (1971). Hedonic relativism and planning the good society. In M.H. Appley (Ed.), *Social Comparison Processes: Theoretical and Empirical Perspectives*. Washington, D.C.: Hemisphere.

Brickman, P., Coates, D., & Janoff-Bulman, R. (1978). Lottery winners and accident victims: Is happiness relative? *Journal of Personality and Social Psychology*, *36*, 917–927.

Diener, E., Horowitz, J., & Emmons, R.A. (1985). Happiness of the very wealthy. *Social Indicators Research*, *l6*, 263–274.

Helson, H. (1964). *Adaption-Level Theory*. New York: Harper & Row.

Schulz, R., & Decker, S. (1985). Long-term adjustment to physical disability. *Journal of Personality and Social Psychology*, *48*, 1162–1172.

Solzhenitsyn, A. (1963). *One Day in the Life of Ivan Denisovich*. Harmondsworth: Penguin.

Wills, T.A. (1981). Downward comparison principles in social psychology. *Psychological Bulletin*, *90*, 245–271.

Chapter 7

Beck, A.T. (1976). *Cognitive Therapy and the Emotional Disorders*. New York: Meridian.

Ellis, A. (1978). What people can do for themselves to cope with stress. In C.Cooper and R.Payne (Eds.), *Stress at Work*. Chichester: Wiley.

Fordyce, M.W. (1977). Development of a program to increase personal happiness. *Journal of Counseling Psychology*, *24*, 511–521.

Palys, T.S., & Little, B.R. (1983). Perceived life satisfaction and the organization of personal project systems. *Journal of Personality and Social Psychology*, *44*, 1221–1230.

Chapter 8

Argyle, M. (1987). *The Psychology of Happiness*. Oxford: Oxford University Press.

Berkman, L.F., & Syme, S.L. (1979). Sociobehavioural determinants of compliance with health and medical care recommendations. *Medical Care*, *13*, 10–24.

Cooper, C. (Ed.) (1982). *Stress at Work*. Chichester: Wiley.

Grossarth-Maticek, G., Eysenck, H.J., & Vetter, H. (1988). Personality type, smoking habit and their interaction as predictors of cancer and coronary heart disease. *Personality and Individual Differences*, *9*, 479–495.

Chapter 9

Diener, E. (1984). Subjective well-being. *Psychological Bulletin*, *95*, 542–575.

Freedman, J.L. (1978). *Happy People*. New York: Harcourt Brace Jovanovich.

Veenhoven, R. (1984). *Databook of Happiness*. Dordrecht: Reidel.

Wilson, W. (1967). Correlates of avowed happiness. *Psychological Bulletin*, *67*, 294–306.

Subject Index